Maintenance of Divine Worship

Howard L. Rice, Jr.

Witherspoon Press
Louisville, Kentucky

Publisher: Sandra Albritton Moak
Editor: Martha Gilliss
Book interior and cover design by Jeanne Williams

First edition

Published by Witherspoon Press
Louisville, Kentucky

Web site address: www.pcusa.org/witherspoon

PRINTED IN THE UNITED STATES OF AMERICA

06 07 08 09 10 11 12 13 14 15—10 9 8 7 6 5 4 3 2 1

Library of Congress Cataloging-in-Publication Data

Rice, Howard L.
  Maintenance of divine worship/Howard L. Rice, Jr.; Martha Schull Gilliss, editor.—1st ed.
p. cm.—(The great ends of the church series)
Includes bibliographical references.
  ISBN 1-57153-055-X (pbk.:alk. paper)
  1. Public worship. 2. Presbyterian Church (U.S.A.)—Doctrines. 3. Reformed Church—Doctrines. I. Gilliss, Martha S. II. Title. III. Series.
  BV15.R53 2005
  264'.05137—dc22   2005020937

Contents

Foreword

Every book is a work of many people who have made the end product possible. Such a situation is certainly true about this book. I received a letter out of the blue asking me to write this part of a series on the Great Ends of the Church. Because it came from the Office of the General Assembly, I was intrigued. I was honored to be asked to participate in the project and delighted to be included along with others whom I admire as writers, such as Catherine Gunsalus Gonzáles and Joe Small. But I was hesitant. Because I had already written a book on worship in the Reformed tradition with my friend James Huffstutler, I was a bit reluctant to write a second. As I went about the task, however, I began to notice many things that I missed in the earlier book. The fluid situation regarding the state of worship today is worth a good deal of attention. It may well be that our ability to rethink our customs and habits regarding worship will determine whether or not our mainstream denominations will make it through this tumultuous century or wither away into irrelevance.

Thus, the issues addressed in this book are those which have come to my attention as one who is both a worshiper and a regular preacher. In my present role as interim president of Cook College and Theological School, I am a guest nearly every Sunday and have had ample opportunity to experience worship in many different congregations of various sizes and situations. They have been great teachers! I have learned to appreciate the difficulty of preparing worship that meets the demands of a diverse population and is still faithful to the tradition. I believe that real heroes out there are doing just that.

Cook College and Theological School has graciously provided me with the time to complete this book. I had agreed to accept this assignment long before I received the phone call that brought me to Cook. The staff and trustees have been supportive, and they deserve a great deal of credit for their encouragement.

Dr. Menno Frose, a volunteer at Cook and a retired sociology professor at Beloit College, has been a good critic and first reader of the manuscript. My wife Nancy has once more played the role of proofreader, and as a former public school teacher, she lets very little escape her critical notice.

To all of these people, the folks at the Office of Theology and Worship, and many more, I owe my thanks. The book would never have happened without all of you.

Howard L. Rice, Jr.
December 2004

Introduction

A number of books have been written about worship, but Howard Rice writes *Maintenance of Divine Worship* especially for Presbyterian Church (U.S.A.) congregations. In this third book addressing the five Great Ends of the Church, Rice places worship in the context of our Reformed confessional heritage. At the same time, he offers practical advice about how congregations can tread the fine line between form and freedom, between tradition and "this is the way we have always done this" on the one hand, and the lure of newer liturgies and practices on the other.

Rice writes this book for the whole congregation, not just for clergy. He writes particularly for those who are interested both in the content and meaning of Reformed forms of worship and in ways that these are beginning to change. Rice makes the case that "the maintenance of divine worship" does not always mean encasing worship in exactly the same forms to which we have been accustomed. Worship fulfills a human need to be united with our Creator. Worship acclaims the presence of God amidst our fluid lives, and focuses on and draws us into God's sovereignty as we meet God together as a congregation. Worship helps form us as Christians, as persons forgiven and called to carry the grace of our Lord Jesus Christ into the world. Moreover, worship is a two-way event. As we worship God, we learn who this God is who claims us as God's own people. In this manner, the most important relationship of our life is nurtured.

Rice emphasizes, "Whatever else a church does, worship is at the very heart of its life." (p. 3) Thus, without a strong worship practice, a church is not only without a vision: it is without a life and will soon die. What is astounding is that God entrusts us ordinary human beings with so much—all that is involved in upholding our end of the relationship with God. Rice shows how worship reenacts the reality of our relationship with God as it moves us through praise, confession, assurance of forgiveness, and hearing the word. These actions form our responsive self-offerings to God. We are able to be God's people, and Christ's body, both apart from the outside world within the sanctuary of worship and in the world as we go out into our neighborhoods. In worship we know exactly who we are. We enact a pattern that reinforces faith and encourages us to adopt values that enable us to resist cynicism and despair in the face of life's hardships. There is a reason Presbyterians use the particular order that we do in our worship. At the same time, as Rice puts it, "there is no single tradition that can stand for all time—all worship patterns are subject to the forces of culture and reflect the situation in which they are engaged." (p. 10) The Holy Spirit breathes new life into human tradition, invigorating practices and introducing new forms of worship that are better able to convey an awareness of the presence of God's grace within the congregation.

Not all change, of course, is good. As Rice makes clear, however, it is the Holy Spirit, speaking through Scripture, who creates both form and freedom in all Christian worship. Sessions (not the pastor!) are responsible for ensuring that worship actually happens and that it is in keeping with the principles of the Directory for Worship.

In this book, Rice provides some tools to help congregations understand the value of our tradition so that we will be able to evaluate changes in worship. He also provides concrete suggestions of things to use and to avoid in worship planning. We are pleased to offer *Maintenance of Divine Worship* as the third volume in the Great Ends of the Church series, knowing that you will find it a lucid and accessible aid in maintaining worship in your congregation!

Martha Schull Gilliss, editor
Congregational Ministries Publishing
April 2005

Why Maintenance of Worship Matters

Whatever else a church does, worship is at the very heart of its life. A congregation can have a fine educational program, do good works in the community, be active in support of missionaries, and provide a wonderful sense of fellowship for its members, but if worship is not at the very center of its life, it is not a church in the fullest sense. Because worship is rooted in the most basic of all human needs—our need for God—worship is basic to what it means to be human. We are created for relationship with God and thus we need to engage in conscious means of attending to God. Augustine of Hippo put it in these words, "You have made us for yourself, and our hearts are restless until they rest in you."[1] Our society is certainly proof of Augustine's insight: North Americans and western Europeans who have abandoned the church in droves are also slipping into hedonism and materialism at levels never before imaginable. Boredom and a sense of fear in the face of the possibility of chaos or death drives people to the many forms of distraction that the modern world provides, including forms of fundamentalism that flourish in the place of traditional religion. Some of us can quite readily lose ourselves in a football game on television or in a film with car crashes and gore. Others can lose themselves in a Pentecostal worship service or by watching a televangelist. We can certainly lose our fears, at least momentarily, by using alcohol or drugs, prescription or illegal. Our culture provides a great many means of escape and does so because many people feel the need for escape from the lives they are leading.

To deny our need for relationship with God is to deprive ourselves of the strength of rootedness. When we ignore God, we are less than we were meant to be and prey to all the distortions of humanity that fill the pages of our daily newspapers and television evening news. Worship keeps us human because worship keeps us reminded of who we really are and to whom we truly belong. Worship is a means of maintaining and restoring the image of God in us, enabling us to function as people who know who we are. Worship can enable us to be free from the various false identities that we wear like masks to seek protection from our fear of our real selves. Worship provides us with what the *Book of Order* describes as "an awareness of God's grace and claim upon [our] lives."[2] It is the grace of God that gives us the courage to admit our real identity with all the blots and stains we know are there. That grace, which we experience through the life and work of Jesus Christ, is the ground of our true identity because it frees us from fear and enables us to dare to live as the people of God. When we worship, we can be truly honest because worship is a means of grace in which we act out the meaning of our salvation. It is a means by which we apprehend the grace that makes us whole and brings us glimpses of the eternal life that begins in the here and now and lasts into eternity.

Worship is one of several means of grace given to us as Christians to enable us to discover that which we might otherwise deny or fail to notice: that God loves us, forgives us, and opens new possibilities for us because we are claimed by the God who comes to us in Jesus of Nazareth. Such grace is experienced both in private and in community. The Westminster Confession of Faith puts it this way: "The light of nature showeth that there is a God, who hath lordship and sovereignty over all; is good, and doeth good unto all; and is therefore to be feared, loved, praised, called upon, trusted in, and served with all the heart, and with all the soul, and with all the might."[3] We worship because in a sense we must. It was the insight of John Calvin that, tarnished though we may be because of the condition known as "original sin," we still know enough about God to be driven either to fear and idolatry or to a proper reverence and respect for that source of all life.

We worship in private when we pray, meditate, read and study Scripture, or engage as individuals in acts of service to others. We also gather with others in communities to share our faith together. Both in private and in public worship, we are attentive to what God has to say to us, we respond in praise and gratitude to God's gifts to us, and we hold up our needs and concerns as well as those of the world to God in prayer.

Private worship provides the necessary seedbed of deep faith from which public worship springs. Private worship stills our busy minds, calms our anxious spirits, and prepares us for the experience of joining with others. If we only worship in public, we are likely to be weak in what we have to bring to private worship. A deeply personal faith is the engine that fuels our spiritual energy and makes public worship a living reality.

Public worship keeps our private devotions from becoming self-centered. When we worship in public, we have to let go of some of our own particular needs and desires in order to participate with others. We can't have it all our own way and that is good for us, for, left to our own preferences, we might well devise a god of our own making rather than be brought before the true God.

If we never worship in public and are content with a private devotional life, we are not likely to experience challenges that make us grow, nor are we likely to have our horizons broadened beyond the immediate purview of our family and community. We need both the personal and the communal in our lives in order to live fully in Christ. If we worship only in public, we risk becoming shallow in our devotional life, and worship becomes a formality to be repeated without much heart in it. To skip private worship is to shortchange our spiritual lives and freight public worship far too much. By itself, one hour or a little more a week simply cannot sustain us in faith for the trials and duties of life.

Public worship matters because it is the one time in the week when God's people gather to acknowledge God's presence in the world and in our lives, to remember our faith, to act out its meaning, to celebrate the good news in Christ, to respond to God's claim on our lives, and to receive the blessing of God. We worship because without worship we forget our identity and begin to believe the lies all around us: the false promises of advertising and the lure to accumulate more possessions. Without God, we are less than fully human. Because God created us in God's own image, we are never more truly happy than when we are acting out our identity in praise, thanksgiving, and acts of commitment. When we worship, we are most fully the people God intends us to be. As the church, we never act more like church than when we worship. It is not possible to imagine a church of any kind that does not gather for worship.

It is impossible to live the Christian life in isolation from God and from the community of faith that is the body of Christ on earth. Even the solitary individual who is at prayer or reads the Bible is connected to the community of faith, which preserves the Scriptures and passes the faith on from generation to generation. The Christian life is too difficult to live by ourselves; our lives are filled with too many temptations and problems. We easily get weighed down by troubles, discouraged by events about which we can do little, frustrated by humiliations and defeats, and discouraged by the failures of our best intentions. It is not difficult to become so discouraged by the failures of our best efforts that we become bitter and cynical. For all these reasons, the Christian life cannot be a do-it-yourself task. We need all the help we can find. Those who act as if worship is a luxury for certain special occasions are running the grave risk of discovering that they have isolated themselves from God and from the spiritual resources necessary for vital faith. Life has a way of draining us of our sense of the holy. We get busy with the everyday tasks of life and preoccupied with work and the tasks necessary for our survival.

Our confessional heritage is clear about the need for the church. The Scots Confession is unswerving in its conviction: "Out of this Kirk there is neither life nor eternal felicity. Therefore we utterly abhor the blasphemy of those who hold that men who live according to equity and justice shall be saved, no matter what religion they profess."[4] The Westminster Confession of Faith moderates that claim somewhat, saying that the church is the means "through which men are ordinarily saved and union with which is essential to their best growth and service."[5] Simply by adding the one word "ordinarily," the Westminster divines accepted the possibility that God may have other means to bring people to salvation in addition to the church, however broadly defined the church may be. Yet, the point must not be lost that the church is not one choice among other choices for Christians. We need the guidance and correction of others, and we need the encouragement to follow Jesus that public hearing of the Word proclaimed regularly provides.

To worship is above all to remember. We forget all too easily in our rush to succeed, to live up to our ideals, or in the temptation to compromise those ideals in order to get ahead or to make a difference in the world. Even in doing good, we can lose touch with our true nature. We begin to think that it is our own efforts that have brought us our blessings, and we take pride in our achievements without ascribing thanksgiving to the source of all our blessings. We become jaded to the holy, focused upon what we can do ourselves, forgetful of the blessings bestowed on us by God, and out of touch with who we really are.

Our true identity is never discovered without taking our spiritual nature seriously. It is a natural outgrowth of the movement away from church attendance in our nation that people sense an inner emptiness which they seek to fill in other ways, from cultic practices to new forms of "spirituality." Whenever we try to live without God, we end up with a sense of lostness and confusion. That inner vacuum will be filled one way or another. Too often in the modern Western world, what replaces a faith rooted in the tradition of Jesus is a vague form of spirituality that tries to have blessings without any effort, any challenge, any involvement on our part. Spirituality can become a form of cheap grace, which New Age spirituality offers, a faith that is self-centered without any correcting influence, and thus completely of our own creation.

At the heart of most of our human failings is forgetfulness. To remember is to put together that which has fallen apart, to put together what has been lost or broken. The broken members of each of our lives need to be brought together into a wholeness. Thus, remembering is more than reflecting intellectually upon the themes of worship (praise, thanksgiving, confession, and dedication). Remembrance is discovering our identity and being restored to be the people God meant us to be.

We remember what is broken and what needs to be repaired in our lives. We remember our fears and failures, the people from whom we are alienated and the ways we have disappointed ourselves, our sense of being distant from God—in short, we remember who we have become in both sorrowful contrition and in grateful thanks, often at the same time. Thus, worship is the primary way of connecting us to God, the ultimate reality. We are restored to our true identity by being in communion with God. We worship, not primarily to be a pleasant, caring community, although that may be true of our experience. We worship, not to feel better, though that may happen, nor to build better communities or healthier churches, though we may, in fact, do just those things. We worship not even to become more moral human beings or to have happier and more peaceful families. Worship is not intended for these purposes. It is not for our sakes that we engage in the acts we recognize as public worship. We worship to focus upon God and to respond to God, and all of the other good things that happen to us and among us are side products of the primary purpose. Because we worship, we may be healthier, have more loving families, be motivated to care more deeply about the poor or take up an unpopular cause, but these are not the reason for worship. They are the by-products.

Unique among the Great Ends of the Church, worship is the only one that makes no sense without God, precisely because worship is where connection with God takes place. That is why worship must be the core of the church's identity. If churches do not engage in this unique ministry, who will? We are about providing means by which people can come into fellowship with God, and therefore worship is vital to the life of the church. Every church building is itself a reminder of the presence of God. If a congregation is not rooted in worship, it may fall into the trap of following the other Great Ends and doing good things but without a sense of God to make those good deeds alive and life-changing. Inasmuch as the church becomes a social club, a welfare organization, or even a concert hall, a church ceases to be alive and becomes a museum to the past. After all, everything else we do can be done by someone else, but not worship.

Worship—whether it is called traditional or contemporary—is always about preserving an ancient tradition. By its very nature, worship has a conservative function. We have a very old story that is the vehicle for our faith, and that story needs to be told over and over in each generation. Some wise soul once said that Christian faith is always only one generation from extinction. Every aspect of worship serves to remind us of our particular sacred story, to reinforce its meaning, and to articulate its consequences in our daily lives, thus providing the guidance we need for making the hard decisions we all face. We hear that sacred story read in Scripture; we sing it in hymns and anthems; it is interpreted for us in sermon, acted out in sacraments and rituals, and expressed in our prayers. The story of God's dealings with the Hebrew people and the story of Jesus and his ministry make up the two essential components of that basic story. If we stray from that story, no matter how successful and interesting, entertaining and alive our worship may be, it no longer serves the essential purpose of Christian worship.

Thus, the third Great End, or purpose, of the church is the "maintenance of divine worship."[6] It is prior to the others in the sense that it must come first—in order for the others to be possible or make any kind of sense. It is possible to exhibit the kingdom of heaven, or the rule of God, without being faithful believers. Other good examples of loving communities exist. It is possible to practice social righteousness apart from the Christian faith tradition. Many good people do. We can provide shelter, nourishment, and spiritual fellowship at some level without a deep connection to God. Witness the wonderful "fellowship" activities in many churches and secular organizations that have no Christian content at all. We can preserve the truth in the spirit of good philosophers who are on a search. We can even proclaim the gospel without much personal sense of being in the presence of God. The church can do all these good things and yet have no heart for that which is at its base. People today really do notice that absence and pass the church by in their search for God.

In worship, we preserve something precious. The dictionary defines "preserve" in a way that is often understood negatively: "to keep from harm, damage, danger, or evil" or "to keep from spoiling or rotting."[7] In fact, the faith has been preserved for us by previous generations who have sought to interpret it in their own times and have also tried to keep the core of the faith pure. Their faithfulness makes it possible for us to possess the gift of faith in our time and to act as conduits for passing that faith on to future generations. Our Presbyterian *Book of Confessions* is a record of the ways our ancestors in the faith have sought to be faithful in their own respective times. Each of these confessional standards speaks with different accents because the issues have not been the same in each century. *The Book of Order* makes it clear that the role of our confessions is to preserve the faith and to maintain the integrity of tradition from generation to generation: "The creeds and confessions of this church reflect a particular stance within the history of God's people. They are the result of prayer, thought, and experience within a living tradition."[8]

The faith is also best maintained in each generation through worship, which is itself a kind of active process of collective remembering. When we worship, we are reminded of all that has shaped our faith, how it has been understood in different situations, and the ways it has led previous generations of Christians to act responsibly in the world. Thus, worship is preserving what is lasting in our own faith. It is not preservation of all that has been done by those who came before us. Otherwise, we Presbyterians would still be limited to singing the Psalms without accompaniment, to hour-long sermons, or even to a Latin mass. In each generation, worship changes because we experience the faith in the forms of our own society. We maintain the traditions of worship by making adaptations that reflect our own time in history. We are not out to correct the mistakes of those who have gone before us because we are smarter or more insightful than they were, but we are about the task of seeking to be faithful in our own way, using our own thought forms, our own understandings of how communities gather, and even our own interpretation of Scripture.

To maintain something requires preserving its integrity and is always a task of great responsibility. We maintain our freedom as a nation at great cost in lives, and it is something we are called to preserve when that freedom is threatened. The maintenance of worship costs us something also. We participate in the rituals and forms of our faith on a regular basis, spending time to keep ourselves reminded of what it means to be Christians. We offer our gifts of money and time to help to make worship possible. Worship is a major part of every congregational budget: the cost of the pastor's salary, the organist and choir director, the utilities for keeping the worship space warm or cool, the janitorial expense of caring for and cleaning that space. Worship is not free! When we worship we give our time when we might be doing other things, we give our attention even when distractions fill our minds, we give ourselves for the sake of community by letting go of our own agenda so that the needs of others may be expressed.

The word "preserve" has always had special meaning for me, because I recall how hard my mother worked to put up preserves every fall. She bought what seemed to be an endless supply of fresh fruit and vegetables, cooked them slightly, put them in sterilized jars, plunged in boiling water, sealed them tightly, and wiped the jars clean. She did all of this hard work in the heat of early autumn to make sure that no spoiling happened in the jars, no air seeped in to cause mold. As a result, her preserves would last until the jars were opened and we ate the products throughout the winter. Even now, I can see row after row of the results: gleaming jars of pickles, peaches, berries, jams, and jellies, enough to last until next summer's crops were available. Mother preserved with great effort and struggle what had been grown one summer in order to feed her family.

Unlike that kind of preserving, or the dictionary definition, preservation is not simply keeping something from being touched by the world. Too often the word "preserve" suggests something stored away and kept pure, like preserved artifacts in a museum. Worship of the church is always affected by culture, by the events and forces that shape those who look for guidance and help. In the beginning of *The Book of Confessions,* there is an introductory article prepared by the Committee on the Confessional Nature of the Church. Referring to the confessions, the article states: "Confessions address the issues, problems, dangers, and opportunities of a given historical situation. But confessions are related to their historical situation also in another way. Even when their writers have believed they were formulating Christian truth valid for all time and places, their work has been directed not only to but limited by their particular time and place."9 Everything said there about confessions can be said about worship. There is no single tradition that can stand for all time—all worship patterns are subject to the forces of culture and reflect the situation in which they are engaged.

People who insist upon doing things in a familiar way in the name of tradition often forget that worship has to be constantly changing in order to be vital and alive. Worship must always use the language of the people (not just the words, but the idioms also) so that it can make the connection between the faith once delivered to the saints and the people present on any given occasion. Just as Elizabethan English has no particular holiness, so also some of the traditional forms we have inherited are no longer meaningful in our world. Even the practice of passing the offering plate when most people pay their pledge monthly because they are paid monthly may need to be reexamined. For us as Christians, maintenance means keeping something alive rather than protecting it from contamination with the world.

Every service of worship is always a delicate balance between adaptation, being able to let go of the familiar in the need to keep the faith meaningful, on the one hand, and holding fast to forms although they may seem obscure to faith, on the other. We keep this balance in order to preserve, and thus protect, patterns out of the past because they are believed to be a necessary part of the gospel itself. There are, of course, some essential elements that must be preserved. Almost no one, would, for example, suggest that the Scripture no longer be read in worship. We do, however, argue about which of the various translations available is most suitable for worship. The task of pastors is to read and interpret Scripture (the old story itself) so that it can be understood by people who may not be familiar with it, as well as by those who need to hear it again and again. In the sixteenth century John Calvin rejected the medieval lectionary in favor of reading and preaching the Gospels in sequence, one section of a Gospel (Matthew, for example) after another until the whole Gospel was covered. He did this because he believed that taking passages out of context was to expect more familiarity with Scripture than was, in fact, present in his day.

Thus, in order to preserve what is most important, pastors may have to make adaptations so that worship can be alive and meaningful in every particular situation. To expect urban dwellers to worship in the same way that rural people do is to be unfair to those whose life experience is very different. Too often we have confused faithfulness with honoring the way "it has always been done" and have frozen certain aspects of worship from the past as sacrosanct even when they no longer serve to communicate.

Our approach to Scripture today, for example, must acknowledge that biblical illiteracy is very common among even very active church members. However pastors choose their lessons, whether by using the Common Lectionary or some other means, they need to take for granted that many people need help to understand the stories and have trouble making sense out of them. The modern lectionary is presented more in sequence than was true in Calvin's day, so it is possible to read through a Gospel with the context of the previous lesson in the minds of the listeners.

There are other ways of helping to make the bridge. A reading may be introduced by a brief commentary to place it in context and help people to understand how it fits into the whole biblical witness. Even such a simple act as printing or announcing the pages in the Bible from which the text is to be read so that people can follow along is a way of recognizing that people need assistance. While they may not know how to find Malachi or 1 Corinthians, they are reluctant to admit their ignorance out of embarrassment.

Musical illiteracy is equally widespread in our culture. Most people no longer make music at home, singing around the piano. Instead, many gather around the television set and stare at it, seeking to be entertained. They bring the same mentality to worship, seeking entertainment out of the service and putting very little of themselves into it. Watch the singing in most churches and you can see people who don't even open the hymnal or pretend to sing. They are listening and perhaps finding blessing in the voices of their fellow worshipers, but they are not attempting to make a contribution themselves. Without giving up on hymn singing, pastors must admit that the challenge is real, and ways must be found to meet the needs of those who worship. They can choose a hymn of the month, have the choir introduce an unfamiliar hymn, or have a soloist sing it for the first time. Hymns can be sung with liveliness and need not be sung as dirges. Sometimes, simply singing a hymn at a faster pace can rescue a dull hymn. Repeating familiar hymns is also a way to enhance singing. Every congregation has its own hymnal within the official one. Some hymns are sung regularly and others rarely or never. Worship leaders must make an effort to use hymns that people do know as much as possible and be careful not to introduce too much new music into any single service.

Even the makeup of the bulletin may discourage some people from active participation. Refrains and responses should be printed in the bulletin. It would be quite helpful if the hymns to be sung were bookmarked ahead of time by faithful deacons or ushers, so that the pages could be easily and quickly found. Adequate instruction should be provided for every part of the service, assuming as little as possible.

Every worship service is an occasion for those who are very comfortable and familiar in church to welcome those who may be new and somewhat intimidated by the whole idea of coming to church.

Above all, maintaining divine worship requires that each generation learn to appreciate the ancient tradition in a new and fresh way. Thus, all worship must be contemporary whether it is called that or not, and every service must be traditional because it bears an ancient message and tries to make it as real today as it was in earlier centuries. We maintain worship when we make it as alive as possible so that people want to return. We maintain worship when we allow the power of the ancient story to ring true for people today, to have meaning for their lives and application to what they do when they leave the place of worship. Worship cannot take place as though in a safe cocoon, removed from the world and the lives people lead from Monday through Saturday. An important question pastors and worship planners need to ask about every element of worship is, "What does it mean today to this congregation?" Worship is part of life, not something removed from it. Even in the same nation and the same historical time, different communities face different questions, and thus their worship will not always be the same. There is a necessary place for diversity.

The last phrase in this Great End is "of divine worship." We gather to worship God, not ourselves, our nation, our ideals, not our splendid sense of family, not our achievements or our plans. We worship the One who is beyond us, and whose ways will remain, at some level, mysterious to us. God is our reason for gathering! At its core, worship is about connection and fellowship between human beings and God. It is about the spiritual life at its fullest, for worship nourishes our souls uniquely among human activities. It does this in explicit ways and in more subtle ones as well. We are shaped by what we do in worship; our souls are different because worship is a means of grace, a way by which the Spirit of God can be apprehended. We may attend worship with one set of expectations but have something else take place that we did not expect. We never know where God will meet us when we worship: we may sense the presence of God in the music, the sermon, the prayers, the hug of a neighbor, singing a hymn, or in the bread broken. However it happens, we are touched at a level far beyond the rational—the holy presence is too magnificent to comprehend.

At those times when we remain distant from what is going on and do not sense the holy, it may be that we came with too much on our minds and that we were distracted, or even because the service was not designed to meet us that day. Planners of worship can so easily forget that every person who attends worship on a given occasion is not in a good spirit, full of joy and thanksgiving. Some are saddened by recent loss or other grief, others may be experiencing the confusion of temptation or the conflict of a difficult decision that needs to be made.

Ideally, worship is designed for such a variety of human needs. There are many possible reasons for some of us to be untouched or unmoved by a particular service. However, if we do not quit expecting something important to happen in worship, God's living presence will touch us. People attend church services with this (often unexpressed) need. However unable they may be to express that hope, they wish that they might have such an encounter. I fear that they are often disappointed and join the ranks of wistful seekers who have given up on the church.

Thus, the preservation of worship is the living encounter between the tradition and the contemporary world. To go too far in either direction is dangerous. We can lose the tradition completely in the effort to be relevant, or we can be so concerned about keeping the tradition that we make it incomprehensible or capable of gross misunderstanding. Finding that balance is never easy, but our charge as Reformed Christians is to do just that.

Notes

1. Augustine, *Confessions, A New Translation,* trans. Henry Chadwick (New York: Oxford University Press, 1992), 1, i.
2. *Book of Order, The Constitution of the Presbyterian Church (U.S.A.),* Part II (Louisville: Office of the General Assembly, Presbyterian Church (U.S.A.), 2004/2005), W-1.1002. (Hereafter *Book of Order.*)
3. The Westminster Confession of Faith, in *The Book of Confessions, The Constitution of the Presbyterian Church (U.S.A.),* Part I (Louisville: Office of the General Assembly, 1999), 6.112. (Hereafter *The Book of Confessions.*)
4. The Scots Confession, in *The Book of Confessions,* 3.16. An alternate reading: ". . . who hold that men and women who live . . ."
5. The Westminster Confession, *The Book of Confessions,* 6.141. An alternate reading: ". . . who hold that men and women are ordinarily saved . . ."
6. *Book of Order,* G 1-0200.
7. *Webster's New World College Dictionary,* 2nd edition, s.v. "preserve."
8. *Book of Order,* G-2.0500.
9. *The Book of Confessions,* xv.

Questions for Discussion and Reflection

1. Why do you attend worship? What kinds of needs does it satisfy for you?

2. How does worship help you to remember what is most important in your life?

3. Can you think of a time when a worship service seemed quaint and irrelevant? If so, what made it seem that way?

4. How does public worship enhance your private devotional life?

5. Do you believe that you can live without regular worship? Why or why not?

6. Have you ever attended a service of worship in which the effort to be modern and contemporary obscured the tradition so that you were left feeling empty?

7. Think about the meaning of the word "preserve." How do you think the worship services you attend preserve the faith?

8. How do you think that the Scripture lessons are chosen in your congregation? Do they seem to be in any particular order?

9. Do you feel motivated to live a more loving life by participating in worship?

The Elements of Worship

All worship is made up of certain elements that may look quite different in various traditions but are very much the same in purpose and intent. These elements include: proclamation and interpretation of a sacred text, prayer (silent, spoken, or sung), adoration, praise, confession, thanksgiving, petition, the offering of self and gifts to God, certain actions that enact the meaning of the sacred text using physical elements, and some ways of making a connection with the wider world beyond the immediate community that is gathered. These same elements are present in Presbyterian worship and in the worship of all Protestant churches, as well as in Roman Catholic and Eastern Orthodox worship. They are also present in the worship of Jews, Muslims, Buddhists, Sikhs, and Hindus, among others. It is not the elements themselves that distinguish our particular form of worship as Presbyterians or even as Christians, but the proportion of time devoted to them, the way they are structured in the order of service, the way in which they may be accomplished, and the particular meaning we ascribe to them. Reading from the Qur´an and reading from the Bible are both examples of proclamation of a sacred text, but the meaning ascribed to the action is very different. Even in different Christian traditions, breaking of the bread in Holy Communion may look the same but have very different meanings.

It is important to look at these elements to see why it matters that we understand their meaning and how we may best express it. In his book *The Future of Protestant Worship,* Ronald Byars reduces all the various elements to three basic elements: book, bath, and meal. To these he adds a fourth: the service of others, especially those most needy.[1] Most of what we do in worship can be contained in one of these four categories.

Book: The Word

At the heart of all Presbyterian worship is the Word of God, which is proclaimed and interpreted. The Word is, of course, first of all Jesus Christ, who is the living, incarnate Word of God and the center of all our worship. Thus, worship is Christ-centered both in name and in intent. We seek to follow Jesus as our master and Lord and, therefore, we need to understand him, to hear him address us in our various life situations, and to sense his presence as strengthening and encouraging. Whatever else worship may accomplish, its primary purpose is to proclaim Christ in ways that enable us to meet him in sacred encounter and to become better able to be obedient to him in our lives. We proclaim Christ by reading Scripture, which is our best witness to him. The Directory for Worship makes clear the centrality of Scripture in Presbyterian worship: "The Scriptures shall be read and proclaimed. Lessons should be read from both Testaments. Scripture shall be interpreted in a sermon or other form of exposition."[2] The use of "shall" means that this is a requirement for worship. Thus, we cannot say that we truly worship without both the reading and interpretation of Scripture. The requirement is clear and points to our Reformed tradition of insistence upon the centrality of Scripture.

The reading and interpretation of Scripture is central for us because we believe that in the spoken word and the word interpreted we are most likely to meet the risen Christ. Martin Luther once called Scripture the "cradle of Christ" because he understood that the sacred texts are the location for our encounter with the Risen One; and he saw that in order to find Christ, we need to look at what he said and did and what the witnesses to his life and teaching reported about him, as well as how the earliest believers understood the meaning of his life, death, and resurrection. As Presbyterians, we also appreciate the value of the Hebrew Bible as the context for understanding Jesus and the spiritual setting out of which he came and upon which he built. Cut off from that witness, we have a tendency to reduce Christian faith to a very individualized, personal matter with little social meaning. The Hebrew prophetic tradition keeps us honest and socially responsible, as does the story of God's dealings with Israel in which the faithfulness of God is demonstrated again and again. The reason why Presbyterians do not rise for the reading of the Gospel lessons is that we want to bear witness to the fact that all Scripture is inspired by God and there are no levels of scriptural value. The same Lord is revealed in the totality of Scripture, and thus, if we were to stand for the Gospel reading, we should stand for the reading of all Scripture.

Presbyterians have a long tradition, dating back to the Westminster Assembly of Divines, who met at Westminster Abbey in the 1640s, of using a reading from both the Hebrew Scriptures and the New Testament. The Directory for Worship strongly suggests that practice today. That traditional twofold reading has been augmented by the use of the Common Lectionary in many congregations and thus to an increase in the number of lessons: a Gospel text and an epistle text are read, a Psalm is used in one form or another (sung or spoken), and the Hebrew Scriptures are also used. In the course of the three-year cycle, the lectionary introduces most of the Bible to the congregation and expands their appreciation of the depth and variety of Scripture. Calvin preached from only one Gospel lesson on Sundays, but he had opportunity to preach from other parts of the Bible during the week at services held daily both morning and evening. In the modern world, we focus our energy and time on the Sunday morning service almost exclusively, and thus we need the variety of readings that the lectionary provides.

A significant problem with the use of several texts is that reading without interpretation can cause confusion and even misunderstanding in the minds of the hearers. Most people who attend worship are not well versed in Scripture and do not have much background for understanding the text. Thus, the pastor or reader (lector) may need to offer a brief explanation of the text as introduction to the reading. In spite of this problem, the use of the lectionary prevents a narrow selection of texts that are easy to hear and interpret, and thus the editing of Scripture to suit our wants. Every preacher has favorite texts that can become a steady diet for the people instead of the whole gospel. The lectionary also gives us a base for ecumenical worship with those of other traditions who also use these texts. The lectionary enables everyone to read the texts and meditate upon them during the week prior to worship, especially when the texts for the coming week are announced ahead of time.

The sermon may, of course, include more than one text, but the effort to make two or more texts fit with each other may be an exhausting intellectual puzzle that bears little fruit in the lives of the people, except to prove how scholarly the pastor is. Fortunately, the Common Lectionary offers readings that provide context for each text by using a particular book of the Bible for a series of consecutive readings. For example, a particular Gospel is offered for the better part of a year. Biblical illiteracy can be compensated for by such prolonged use of a single book of Scripture, and one sermon can build upon another so that people come to recognize the uniqueness of each particular book.

The preaching of the Word belongs with the reading of Scripture as a single action, which is preceded by prayer for the illumination by the Holy Spirit. We do not automatically hear what God has to say to us by simple hearing. We are distracted by other matters, influenced by other occasions when we heard the same text read, inhibited by our prejudices about a particular text, or influenced by misunderstandings about the meaning of certain key words. Instead of hearing a word from the Lord, we hear words that bother us, confirm our preconceived ideas, confuse us, or lull us to sleep. We may even hear words that mislead us when, for example, in the story of Jesus' crucifixion, we hear the horrible words from the crowd, "His blood be upon us and upon our children." These words have been the basis of much anti-Semitism and have led to pogroms in which Jews have been singled out and labeled as "Christ killers."

Every preacher has preached on occasions when a hearer failed to get the point of the sermon and commented in such a way as to indicate misunderstanding. Such moments are humbling for all preachers. Thus, preachers need the Holy Spirit to work in the people to silence the voices that cause them to fail to pay attention and to listen with care to what is being read and preached. Calvin introduced this prayer for right hearing in his Genevan worship services because he had such a high view of Scripture that he wanted to be sure that people were enabled truly to hear. The prayer for illumination functions rather like the Great Prayer in the service of Holy Communion. Both prayers invoke the Holy Spirit, the former upon the hearers and the latter upon the action of the table. The minds of the hearers need to be attentive to the message that God imparts both through the word read and the word interpreted. It is all too easy for people to attend church but have their attention elsewhere. We all need the power of the Holy Spirit to listen attentively.

The order of worship should always demonstrate that the Word read in Scripture and the Word preached is a single action. Anything that breaks the connection and interrupts the unity of the Word and Sacrament should be chosen with great care and reluctance. For example, a hymn or choral anthem may be sung that restates the message of the text and prepares us to hear the sermon, or a psalm may be used between two readings so as to make a bridge between them. There may be occasions when use of a Bible translation other than that of the authorized pulpit Bible is necessary, but ordinary use of the pulpit Bible is a way of emphasizing the unity of Scripture and sermon, as does the practice of both reading and preaching from the pulpit itself. If other readers are to be used, they should normally also move to the pulpit for their readings. If the pastor chooses not to use the pulpit for preaching, it is still important that he or she demonstrates the unity of Scripture and sermon, perhaps by reading the Bible from the place where the preaching takes place.

The sermon has had a long and varied practice among Christians, inherited from Jesus. Beginning with the New Testament church, preaching has always been important, although in the pre-Reformation churches of the West, it fell into disuse. Most clergy were neither trained nor competent to preach, so the people came to witness the miracle of the mass without any interpretation of the Word. Scripture was read, but in Latin. However, even in the "Dark Ages" there were always great traveling preachers whose powerful preaching attracted crowds, although their work was often not part of the official worship of the church. The Protestant Reformation sought to restore preaching to its central role in worship. The sermon was often quite lengthy (an hour or longer) in a culture in which there was little competition from other forms of communication. In our contemporary television culture, in which people are used to sound "bites" that limit attention to the twelve to thirteen minutes between commercials, we have little tolerance for long sermons, even for twenty-minute sermons, and people begin to drift away from even the best preaching. Reducing the time of the sermon is both necessary and difficult to accomplish, but it is possible to hone a sermon down to ten to twelve minutes without doing damage to the importance of what is spoken.

Preaching is always a means of interpreting Scripture to the people and begins and ends with the text itself. With rare exceptions, people do not come to hear the pastor's opinions, though it is impossible to leave them out. They do quite rightly expect to hear a "word from the Lord"—some illumination or clarification of the text, some way of bringing the text into their lives and making the ancient words relevant to them. The sermon is always a bridge between the world in which it was produced and the world in which it is heard. Preachers stand between those worlds, holding them in creative tension. They can err on the side of relevance so that the text is nearly ignored or used as a jumping off place for a lecture on a pet subject, but they can also err on the side of focusing upon the text to the exclusion of any point of contact with people's lived experience today, so that they go away wondering what it could possibly mean for them. The balance is difficult to maintain: faithfulness to Scripture and accuracy in presenting its message also provide people with the ability to hear themselves addressed and to receive the tools to build their lives. A faithful sermon provides people with a context of meaning in which to face their questions and difficulties.

The proclamation of the Word is the primary means by which a living sense of the connection between worship and personal and corporate responsibility in the world is demonstrated. This proclamation prevents worship from becoming disconnected with the peoples' lives in the world, and it also works against a privatization of faith, a reduction of faith into a spiritualized experience without consequences for ethical, political, economic, and family life. The Word provides the motivation for taking risks because of faith, it stretches the imagination and it enlivens the conscience.

Bath: Baptism

Water is used in nearly every religion as a sign of cleansing. Hindus bathe in the sacred waters of the Ganges River; Muslims, Buddhists, Jews, and others have rituals of washing to symbolize cleansing before God. Water plays such a vital part in human life that it is to be expected that water is given a central role in worship. For Christians, the bath is baptism. The use of water for baptism is the primary connection of Christians to the nearly universal practice of ritual bathing.

Baptism has a long history. It began as a practice among Jews during the exile in the sixth century B.C. to symbolize joining the community. For a period of time Judaism was quite eager to win new converts, and the moral purity and clear monotheism of Judaism attracted many proselytes. These converts were baptized with water; the men and boys were also circumcised, but it was the act of baptism that became a sacrament for Christianity. Like circumcision, it signified a mark of acceptance and belonging, even though the baptismal mark was invisible. We still refer to baptism as a "sign and seal" of our engrafting into Christ. For Calvinists especially, baptism's connection with circumcision was important. Unlike circumcision, baptism applied to both men and women and was thus a sign of our equality before God.

John the Baptist revived the practice of baptism. He proclaimed a baptism for the forgiveness of sins and invited people to come forward and be lowered into the river water as a sign of their willingness to put aside the ways of sin and be cleansed to rise into new life. The New

Testament church maintained this practice and, like John the Baptist, continued to baptize by immersion. Christians also connected baptism with the reception of the Holy Spirit since the Gospels made it clear that Jesus made this connection (as did John). The early church used both water and oil to signify the Holy Spirit. Oil, symbolizing the Holy Spirit, has been known throughout history as the oil of gladness, traditionally consisting of olive oil scented with a hint of perfume, such as balsam. Thus, baptism has a variety of meanings, all of which come out of its history.

Baptism is the welcome into the household of faith given through the use of water and the Trinitarian formula to seal the new member with God's sign of welcome. Whether the water is of enough quantity to resemble a real bath, as with immersion, or a more symbolic sprinkling or pouring, the use of water is essential to represent new life. Just as water refreshes us when we are parched, it cleanses us when we are soiled. Water is the source of life; all of us come from the water of the womb and thus baptism symbolizes our common origin. Water is part of the natural world—a gift of God—and its use in baptism should be generous enough to demonstrate that water is important. In the history of our faith, water represents God's gift of creation and redemption. The creation story of Genesis explains the beginning of earth as coming out of the primeval waters. The people of Israel were led from slavery in Egypt through the waters of the sea to their freedom, and Jesus was led out of the Jordan River to begin his ministry.

To be washed is a wonderful way to express welcome. Sufficient water should be used, perhaps poured publicly from a pitcher into the font before the sacrament. The pastor may dip his or her hand into the water and scoop some up, letting it fall back into the font so that water is visible and its sound can be heard. Historically, it is common practice for the pastor to sprinkle or pour water over the candidate three times using the traditional words "in the name of the Father, and of the Son, and of the Holy Spirit." The person being baptized should be wet, at least on the head. A towel can be put around the neck of an adult to protect the clothing and afterward given to the newly baptized person as a symbol and reminder of his or her baptism. It might be embroidered with a cross, the date, and the name of the person.

Whether we are too young to remember or of mature years, the welcome of baptism is just as real. The newborn child is welcomed into the household of faith, enrolled as a baptized member of the congregation, and treated as one of the family. Those who approach baptism having made a decision to do so are also welcomed and included. They become active members of the church, and in most baptismal rituals they are greeted warmly by the members of the church. Sometimes a special reception is held for them as part of coffee hour.

At whatever age it is received, baptism is a sign of welcome into the household of faith. However we do it, baptism is always a public event. The congregation is gathered to receive this new member of the family of Christ. Private baptisms do not make sense except in special situations, and even then, elders should join the pastor to represent the gathering of the whole congregation.

Whether it is received as an infant, as a child, or as an adult, baptism is always an act of God. No one ever baptizes himself or herself. Baptism is always something done to us. First of all, baptism is an act of God that proclaims by washing with water the acceptance of the person by God's grace. More than any other act of worship, baptism clearly and dramatically represents and enacts grace. The newborn child in particular has done nothing to warrant grace, is quite unaware of the tenets of the faith, has made no effort of any kind, and is completely without any merit. Yet that baby is accepted by God, included in the covenant of grace, and set upon the way of Christ by sheer grace. Any effort to shift the emphasis from what God is doing to what the person is doing—whether the cute antics of the baby or the testimony of the new believer—is dangerous. Baptism easily seems to become something we do and thus a human accomplishment.

When human achievement or decision becomes central, we take grace from its central place and replace it with human activity. We talk about our decision, our conversion, our study, our faith statements and less about the wonder of what God does for us. Whenever grace is replaced with human works, rebaptism easily becomes an issue. If a person doesn't feel that an earlier baptism was valid because it was without meaning, because it took place in a different denomination, because the pastor was of questionable faith or morality, or any other reason, a second baptism will often be sought to repair whatever was believed to be deficient with the first one. When, on the contrary, the emphasis is very clear that baptism is about what God is doing and has done, then no rebaptism will be necessary or even seriously considered. The Directory for Worship makes the point clear when it defines baptism: "The Sacrament of Baptism, the sign and seal of God's grace and our response, is the foundational recognition of Christian commitment."[3] Every effort to ask for a rebaptism should be discouraged because it takes away from the centrality of grace. The miracle of baptism is that while we are unable to do anything, God reaches out to include us in the covenant community. Before we can ask, God forgives us in advance.

Fortunately, today we have resources for renewing our baptism that can serve to meet the pastoral needs of those who have made significant changes in their lives and need to act out that spiritual renewal. There are other ways to meet the need: When a young child is baptized, it is helpful for the pastor to write that child a letter describing the service. That letter can be read on the anniversary of the baptism so that, as the child grows, his or her baptism will be made very clear. The growing child will be regularly reminded of baptism. Whenever a person is being baptized, an important part of the ceremony is that each baptism is a reminder of our own baptism. Regularly, in prayers, we should be led to consider the grace by which we have been baptized. Such acts will reinforce the importance of baptism for all of us.

Some families do not bring their children to be baptized because they want to give the child a chance to make a personal decision at a time of maturity. While one can appreciate the spirit behind this decision to postpone, we do not postpone other important matters in the child's life until later. We teach very young children boundaries; we teach them what "no" means; we instruct them in manners and morals without hesitation. Why not complete that instruction by this sign of grace?

Along with most other Christians, Presbyterians baptize infants, children, and adults. Baptism is the same sacrament regardless of who receives it. It is always a sign of grace, a welcome, a washing, and the gift of the Holy Spirit. While baptism of believers is clearly the practice of the New Testament church, as the church grew and expanded, children were born in families that had already become Christian, and they were baptized without much controversy. Some worship resources provide separate orders for the baptism of children and use the story of Jesus and the children as a biblical precedent. Our present-day *Book of Common Worship* includes only one order, which can be used for both children and believers to emphasize the oneness of the sacrament. Pastors may adapt the liturgy, however, or utilize other resources such as the Church of Scotland's *Book of Order,* which includes a beautiful order for the baptism of children.

In earlier times, the name of the child was given at baptism. We still put emphasis upon the "Christian name" of the person being baptized and we distinguish the Christian name from the family name. We are all members of the one household and our differences are not important in this moment. The person being baptized is asked his or her name, or the parents or sponsors of one being presented as a candidate are asked, "What is the name of this child?" and they respond as part of the sacramental action.

Baptism has many different meanings. The Directory for Worship lists them: "the faithfulness of God, the washing away of sin, rebirth, putting on the fresh garment of Christ, being sealed by God's Spirit, adoption into the covenant family of the Church, resurrection and illumination in Christ."[4] No single meaning can ever be sufficient to describe what it means to us. We may emphasize one or more of these several meanings but they are all present in every baptism.

Meal: Holy Communion

From the time of the New Testament, Christians have met to share a meal together, even though that meal is largely symbolic. In the beginning, the meal—known as the Lord's Supper or Holy Communion—was a real meal like the Jewish festival of Passover from which it was derived. When the apostle Paul was scolding the Christian community at Corinth, he cited his disgust at their habit of eating without waiting for those delayed by demands of employers. He went so far as to proclaim that they failed to discern the Lord's body in their greed to get to the table first. The body of which he wrote was, of course, the body of the church, which became divided by greed and insensitivity. It may have been Paul's criticism that the Corinthians drank too much and became inebriated at the Lord's Table that contributed to a gradual withdrawal of food and drink from the sacred meal, so that Communion became composed of only the elements of bread and wine, and these in very small quantities.

On the night of his arrest and betrayal, Jesus shared a Passover meal with the disciples in a special room in Jerusalem. As with every Passover celebration, bread and wine were shared along with a meal. The elements of bread and wine are symbols; they represent the history of the people of Israel so that the experience is both worship and teaching. That last supper of Jesus became a defining moment for the disciples. After the death and resurrection of Jesus, they remembered and repeated that meal over and over. The disciples looked back and saw more than the signs of the exodus in that meal. They saw the crucified body and blood of Jesus and were reminded of his ongoing presence with them. Thus, Christians from those early congregations on have experienced the living Christ when they have shared the meal together, and, like the disciples on the road to Emmaus, they have recognized Jesus in the breaking of the bread and have been empowered to face the risks and trials of life because they have known his power in them and among them.

From the time of the earliest Christian communities until the Protestant Reformation, Holy Communion was celebrated every Lord's Day and even daily. In spite of connections between Passover and Communion, the most obvious difference is that Passover is celebrated annually and Communion is repeated frequently. In their effort to be faithful to the incarnation by the connection between the reality of this world and that of the spiritual world, Christians have insisted upon the use of physical elements that are set apart from an ordinary use for a sacred one. Thus, bread becomes, by the power of the Holy Spirit, the sign of the living body of Christ, and the wine the sign of his blood poured out for the forgiveness of our sins.

How this is so is a mystery that has caused endless controversy. Although the experience of millions of people has been remarkably similar, interpretations of the Lord's Supper have varied widely. Some insist that a miracle of transformation is performed each time the sacrament is celebrated, and the bread actually becomes one with the substance of Christ's body. Others insist that the elements are symbolic, that they only point to a reality beyond themselves. Between these two positions there are many other possible interpretations, and within most Presbyterian congregations there are probably several different ideas about the meaning of Communion going on simultaneously. Some folks insist adamantly that after all, it is "*only* a symbol," forgetting that the really important meanings of our lives are symbolized to enable us to recognize and remember them! A wedding ring is only a symbol. Other people who have a more mystical view see with the eyes of faith that something has taken place that makes them experience the community in a new way as a sacred fellowship that can only be described as "the body of Christ." Still others acknowledge that as they take the elements into their bodies, they experience a sense of indwelling of the risen Christ so that as they leave the service, they can proclaim with confidence that they are carrying Christ with them into their everyday lives. No one of these attitudes is wrong, yet none has the full truth. Because through the centuries of Christian experience so many meanings have become attached to what transpires, it is natural that agreement about how Christ is present remains beyond us all.

The Protestant Reformation began as a protest against the abuses of the medieval church and especially the sacramental system through which the clergy maintained power over the people, dispensing or withholding grace. Luther, Calvin, and the rest of the major reformers all insisted that it was the whole people of God, not just the priest present at the Table, who received grace. Thus, they insisted that both the bread and wine be given to everyone. They insisted that no single explanation of how Christ is present in the elements is sufficient to explain the mystery, and no single method of distributing the elements is completely satisfactory. Although they wanted Communion every Lord's Day, the reaction to excesses in the Catholic Church was such that they could not achieve their goal. People were fearful of the superstitions that had accompanied the sacrament.

One of the ironies of history is that at the time of the Reformation the objection to weekly Communion by Roman Catholics was fear of eating to their own damnation, but that opposition to weekly Communion today comes from those who are mistrustful of symbols and anything mysterious. Thus, many Protestant churches, including most Presbyterians, celebrate Communion monthly or even quarterly. Our focus has become intellectual, directed to interpretation of the Word to the exclusion of sacrament. We build magnificent pulpits from which the Word is to be expounded, but tiny baptismal fonts that are often hidden from view and Communion tables that are anything but central to the life of the congregation, sometimes functioning as "worship centers" for all kinds of activities.

In spite of our Reformed tradition that goes back to John Calvin and our confessional heritage, which includes the condemnation of the point of view that holds that the elements are "bare signs,"[5] we modern Presbyterians have tried to keep symbols at a distance and to reduce their size, importance, and power to transform us. The real point of the Lord's Supper is that it makes us new and vital disciples. It seals the Word, applying it to our hearts so that it reaches us at a place beyond our intellect. We Presbyterians have often been so proud of our academic achievements and anxious about any threat to our intellectual understanding that we have resisted the power of the mystical, the symbolic, and the nonrational. Nowhere is this more evident than our resistance to making the sacraments more central in our lives.

The Service of Others

The fourth element of worship is service to others, especially the poor. This element prevents worship from being so self-centered that it becomes an end in itself. No matter how lovely our worship may be, or even how inspiring, if it does not connect us with the world around us, it fails the test of Christian worship. There is a story, which may be only a fiction, that at the time of the Russian Communist revolution, a synod of the Orthodox Church had been convened to deal with some matter of liturgical propriety. The issue may have been important to those who discussed it, but in comparison to the hunger of the masses and the chaos in the streets, it seems now to be totally irrelevant. Some of our current debates about worship seem similarly out of touch. Worship must connect with the world around us, speak to that world, and be focused upon its needs.

There are three primary symbols of our concern for others: first, the offering of our tithes and gifts; second, the announcements and the prayers of intercession; and third, the charge that sends the congregation out into the world. These may be augmented by a time of concerns expressed by members of the congregation, although most congregations seem reluctant to name these concerns aloud without practice. Even then, they are often limited to those related to immediate family and close friends, which enlarges our boundaries but only a little. Thus, the congregation may need encouragement to make their prayers more expansive, reaching beyond the boundaries of kinship and firsthand community to encompass the world. The Presbyterian publication *The Mission Yearbook for Prayer & Study* is an excellent resource because it provides names and concrete examples of our mission work. It can be a guide for prayer so that people appreciate the breadth of mission while praying for the people we support and the work they do. The traditional pattern for prayers of intercession and petition, sometimes called the prayers of the people, is as follows: first, prayers for the people of the congregation, then for the church around the world, for other denominations and nations, for rulers and all those in authority, and finally for the whole world.

The time of announcements can also help to include concerns in the neighborhood, the community, and the world. We speak about our concern for peace in a time of war, for plenty in a time of want, for health in the midst of sickness. We trust as we offer our concerns that God hears these as forms of prayer and responds, even though we cannot ever understand this mystery. We cannot possibly understand why it is that some people seem to be healed by our prayers and others continue to get sick and die in spite of lots of prayer. Counting the number of people praying is no way to determine who will live and who will die. The mystery of life and death rests with God whose ways are always beyond us.

Announcements can become trivial and far too long without some guidance by the pastor or worship leader. Announcements that affect the life of the congregation are appropriate but not announcements that become advertisements for coming events, even important ones. Once this happens, the pastor is caught in the awkward and unpopular position of saying "yes" to some and "no" to others, or affirming or denying all based on a standard that may be confusing or upsetting to some.

The announcements, prayers, and the offering rightfully go together. We offer our gifts, and they accompany our other actions as part of our response to God. We hear the gospel and we respond in gratitude to that good news. The offering and prayer of dedication that follow are signs of our response to the good news and represent our commitment.

Although many if not most church members make a pledge and pay by the month rather than by the week, worshipers should consider putting something in the plate as a kind of extra-mile giving to demonstrate commitment and to bear witness to that commitment to others. Otherwise, the offering plate may go empty for several rows of pews, making the newcomer feel ill at ease and wondering what is wrong. The music that accompanies the collection of gifts is often the loveliest in the whole worship service. We rightly stand for the presentation of our gifts and frequently sing some version of the "Doxology." Other hymns or hymn verses could be used, such as the following from *The Presbyterian Hymnal:* "Breathe on Me, Breath of God," "Here I Am, Lord," "Just as I Am," "More Love to Thee, O Christ," "O Jesus, I Have Promised," "Take My Life," "We Give Thee but Thine Own." Using the topical index of the hymnal to locate other hymns to use for this presentation can provide some variety that makes this part of the service even more meaningful.

The conclusion of our worship is the charge and dismissal. The dismissal is often a benediction, or blessing, given to the people by the pastor in the name of the triune God: God the Father, Jesus Christ the Son, and the Holy Spirit. The charge is given as a way of connecting what has transpired in worship with the world of struggle, temptation, and confusing decisions that we face once we leave the sanctuary. The charge is an assurance that we go out in the company of the One with whom we had communion in worship. The Lord who calls us together sends us out to serve. Thus, it can be said that our worship is not over simply because we part. As we leave, we take with us the experience we shared and are stronger for it. We are part of a family that disperses into the world but remains a family, however scattered.

Offering, prayers, announcements and charge are all ways to make sure that worship does not become irrelevant to our lives. The more lovely and inspiring it has been, the greater the danger of isolating it from the rest of life. In every Gospel, Jesus' post-resurrection appearances to his disciples have to do with sending them out into the world. He does not appear just to satisfy their spiritual hunger or provide inspiration, but as a vehicle to empower them for service.

Notes
1. Ronald Byars, *The Future of Protestant Worship: Beyond the Worship Wars* (Louisville: Westminster John Knox Press, 2002).
2. *Book of Order,* W-3.3101(1).
3. *Book of Order,* W-3.3602.
4. *Book of Order,* W-2.3004.
5. The Scots Confession, in *The Book of Confessions,* 3.21.

Questions for Discussion and Reflection

1. According to Ronald Byars, worship can be reduced to three basic elements: book, bath, and meal. Do you think that the fourth element is not a basic element? Why or why not?
2. Rice reminds us that Presbyterians consider all of Scripture to be the inspired Word of God. What difference does this make in the way you read the Old Testament? What effect could this have on your interpretation of particular texts?
3. Does your congregation use the Common Lectionary? Based on this experience, discuss the pros and cons that Rice lists. With which do you agree? Disagree?
4. Do you ever pray for guidance by the Holy Spirit as you listen to Scripture? Before you hear (or write) a sermon? Why do you think that it is important to connect the reading of Scripture so closely with the sermon?
5. Name some reasons for using water generously during baptism. What might be some good arguments for full immersion? What might be some against it?
6. Does your congregation do a good job recognizing the two functions of baptism: washing and welcoming? Which is given more attention?

7. Describe the miracle of baptism. Have you ever felt the need, or heard someone else express a need, to be rebaptized? How was that need responded to?
8. How does your congregation celebrate Communion? Does it always celebrate it the same way? If so, do you prefer one way over the other? Why?
9. Explain briefly your understanding of the meaning of Holy Communion. How do you think that it changes the way you live your life?
10. How are prayers for others and self made in your congregation? Who decides the content of the prayer? Does the congregation have input?

Prayer in Worship

3

Because worship is essentially a form of communion with God, prayer is at the very core of all worship in every religious tradition. Prayer is the means that God has given us to speak and to tell our truth to God, to share our joys, dreams, and sorrows with God, and to offer ourselves to God, all in the spirit of Jesus. Communicating with God may also include prayerful actions that are forms of our response to God. For example, joyful sharing of our gifts, talents, or financial resources with others performed as deeds of praise and gratitude are ways to approach God actively in prayer. Prayer is also listening for God to speak to us. Speaking, listening, and acting are all forms of prayer that are part of public worship. Silent prayer may be still fairly rare in most Presbyterian churches but it is not unheard of today. A fourth form of prayer, simply resting in God without words, is often called "meditation." Long ago, John Calvin wrote that the best prayers are often without words. Meditation is letting the mind go blank and then seeing what it is that God may wish to bestow upon us. In wordless meditation, we bring to God our emptiness, asking for nothing but a sense of the personal presence of the Holy One.

Song is another major form of prayer. When prayer is attached to music, the poetry is enhanced, the power of the emotions is strengthened, and the corporate nature of the prayer is realized. We may not always realize the fact, but most hymns and psalms are prayers. We may be so used to singing the hymns that we have forgotten to think of them as prayer, but just consider these favorites: "Abide with Me," "Be Thou My Vision," "Christ of the Upward Way," "Guide Me, O Thou Great Jehovah," "Lead On, O King Eternal," and "Make Me a Captive, Lord." When we are singing these hymns, we are praying together.

The same can be said for our use of the Psalms. Many of them are also prayers, and whether read together in unison or responsively, or set to music, they are a form of sung corporate prayer. In many Reformed denominations today, the use of the sung Psalter is making a comeback after a period in which psalms were considered "old-fashioned." Psalms have been set to wonderful new melodies, so that they may be sung by a cantor with the people singing a refrain that is repeated after a number of verses. In this way the congregation participates in the singing and in the praying. The psalms are a no-nonsense style of prayer. They offer complete honesty to God; often they are full of complaint, and sometimes they are accusatory. Nearly always, however, they come to resolution in a form of thanksgiving and praise.

The Directory for Worship makes the importance of prayer clear: "Prayer is at the heart of worship. In prayer, through the Holy Spirit, people seek after and are found by the one true God who has been revealed in Jesus Christ. They listen and wait upon God, call God by name, remember God's gracious acts, and offer themselves to God. Prayer may be spoken, sung, offered in silence, or enacted."[1] This definition makes it clear how varied prayer can be. It also explains the universality of prayer. People of all religions—even those who do not take part in organized religion—pray.

There are several types of prayer, and these are easily remembered by using the acronym ACTS. A is for adoration, C is for confession, T is for thanksgiving, and S is for supplication. Just about all prayers can be covered by these categories with the possible exception of prayers of dedication and the most common form of prayer in Scripture, the psalms of lament, which are prayers of complaint to God.

Prayers of Adoration

Adoration is prayer that simply pours out its delight to God. Such prayer may not have any particular subject in the sense that it is not thanksgiving for a particular blessing or a response to a gift received from God. It simply celebrates God for being God. Several psalms are of this type, and so are a great many hymns and praise songs. They celebrate the wonder of the mystery of God, the love of God, and the grace of God. Poetry may give expression to this kind of prayer better than prose. Two good examples of hymns of adoration are "Immortal, Invisible, God Only Wise" and "God of the Sparrow." One dates to the nineteenth century, and the other is quite new, but both are examples of rhapsodic praise of God for no specific reason. Other good examples of songs of adoration include many of the praise songs sung frequently at contemporary worship services. In the relatively new Presbyterian alternative hymnal *Sing the Faith*,[2] several good examples can be named: "Awesome God," "Thou Art Worthy," "Father, I Adore You."

Prayer with hands raised to heaven is a form of praise in which posture enacts the mood of prayer and expresses the feelings of adoration. Such a bodily expression is also a link to our common heritage, for it is the posture that was most common among the ancient Hebrews.

Of all forms of prayer, adoration may least require words. A simple exclamation of wonder at a sunset and the silent upward gaze at the magnificence of the sky on a starlit night are both forms adoration in its purest form. Much of this kind of prayer takes place in the natural world when we exclaim over its beauty or wonder at its magnificence. Expressions such as "Ooooo" and "Ahaa" may be the truest words in prayers of adoration.

In addition to traditional hymns of adoration, praise is offered in congregational responses such as the "Gloria," the "Doxology," "The Magnificat," chants such as those from the Iona or the Taizé communities, and other contemporary musical forms. Many of the modern praise songs do nothing more than adore God. Music may be the finest form of praise and adoration of all. A glorious instrumental prelude or offertory can lift our souls in silent praise.

Prayers of Confession

All of us know that we have failed in various ways to live up to what we know we can be. We have failed to fulfill our own dreams for ourselves; we have soiled our souls by deeds of unkindness, thoughtlessness, and even cruelty toward others. We have broken the code of behavior that we know and expect of ourselves. We have betrayed our sense of identity as disciples of Jesus. We carry around our sense of failure by whatever name we may choose to call it. Sin is one scriptural word for "missing the mark" and a good description of how we often feel about ourselves. We have missed the mark of our own high hopes and expectations, and we have let others down, especially those we love and cherish most. Our lives are not what we want them to be because we have allowed them to become distracted by momentary desires and by temptations to sell our standards short or to take short cuts around the moral law in order to save face or to save some money. We have cheated on taxes or we have cheated the Lord of our tithes.

Confession is owning up to our condition; it is a way of telling the painful truth about ourselves. To come before God is to know that we are in the presence of the Holy One before whom all pretense is impossible and all forms of dishonesty are reflected back to us in grim reality. Quite often, our principle form of public confession is a unison prayer that tries to speak on behalf of the whole congregation by using words that are generic enough to include everyone. Such prayers may be used frequently enough that they become so familiar to the people that they can pray them without worrying about getting the words correct.

Following a spoken prayer, it is common to permit a time of silence for all to make their private confessions. It is in this silent confession that we can get more explicit about our failings than we could possibly do corporately. Corporate confession must be somewhat vague so as to include us all, but private confession can name concrete instances in which we know we have sinned. Such silent time needs to be of sufficient length that people can engage in reflection upon their lives. A minute may seem like a long time when nothing is being said, but less time is insufficient for people to collect their thoughts and express them.

Words of assurance of our forgiveness follow so that the confession concludes with a note of grace and the affirmation "We are forgiven." The words need to be spoken forcefully because without this assurance, we tend to hang on tenaciously to our sense of sinfulness.

Hymns of confession are less common than other forms of sung prayer, but sometimes a single verse of a hymn may be a good way to bring music into a time of confession. For example, any verse from "Dear Lord and Father of Mankind" or from "O God of Earth and Altar" would be appropriate at the end of the prayer of confession, as would a single verse of many other hymns. Psalm 51 could be read, sung, or chanted as a confession also. The importance of forgiveness must never be forgotten, however. Otherwise, people are left with only their guilt. Our faith is rooted in the forgiveness of God.

Prayers of Thanksgiving

We all live with blessings taken for granted. Worship is an occasion for remembering and giving thanks for God's goodness to us every day of our lives. Not to be thankful is to be less than fully human. Gratitude is central to a full life; without it we begin to take credit for our blessings or even worse, take them for granted. Our materialistic society tends to cause us to want more and more and be dissatisfied with what we have because it is not good enough, new enough, or big enough. The advertising industry survives by making us vividly aware of what is lacking in our lives so that we want to buy more of what is offered as a way of filling a void. Commercial appeals are carefully crafted to create needs in us so that we will make purchases whether or not we need what we buy. A common commercial for Christmas advertises merchandise for the "person who has everything." Such an acknowledgment makes the case for consumption as an end in itself. When we focus our attention on what we think we need rather than on what blessings we now have, we are not content. Thanksgiving is a means of counteracting the power of dissatisfaction by bringing to mind all the goodness that God has brought about in our lives.

In such a world, there needs to be a place for giving thanks to God as author of our blessings. The old refrain "Count your blessings, name them one by one" is good advice for us all. When we see our lives as gifts, we are likely to sense the many ways in which we are blessed and concentrate more on blessings than upon what is lacking. Thanksgiving thus makes people happier.

Thanksgiving is different from adoration in that it offers up to God specific reasons for our delight. We remember, and thus we give thanks. Prayers of thanksgiving are quite specific as acts of remembrance of what God has done for us; they cite the particular blessings that are reasons for our joy and delight.

The Psalms contain thanksgivings, sometimes mixed with complaints or petitions. The psalmist remembers the goodness of God in the past and draws hope for the present and future from the remembered steadfastness of the Lord. The same can be said of hymns and songs of thanksgiving. They celebrate what God has done and take heart from occasions when we have experienced the goodness of God. Hymns such as "God, Whose Giving Knows No Ending," "Let All Things Now Living," and "Now Thank We All Our God" are good examples of such prayers and expressions of gratitude. One of the favorite praise songs is a thanksgiving, "Give Thanks with a Grateful Heart."

Far less often than a unison prayer of confession congregations offer a unison prayer of thanksgiving. Such a prayer of thanksgiving is provided in the *Book of Common Worship.*

Almighty and merciful God,
from whom comes all that is good,
we praise you for your mercies,
for your goodness that has created us,
your grace that has sustained us,

your discipline that has corrected us,
your presence that has borne with us,
and your love that has redeemed us.

Help us to love you,
and to be thankful for all your gifts
by serving you and delighting to do your will,
through Jesus Christ, our Lord. Amen.[3]

Perhaps it is a failing in much of our worship that thanksgiving has such a minor role. It is often part of the prayers of the people, as they are frequently called. Because all prayer is "of the people," these prayers are more appropriately named prayers of petition and thanksgiving. The worship leader may invite the people to speak aloud or remember silently ways in which they have experienced the goodness of God just as often as they are invited to name concerns. As people are encouraged to give voice to their blessings, their spoken words serve to remind everyone present of the loving provision of God. When someone names a reason for thanksgiving aloud, the people may well respond by using a refrain, "We thank you, O Lord."

The Great Prayer of Thanksgiving or the Prayer of Consecration in the service of Holy Communion is an expression of the thankfulness of the whole people of God for creation, for God's calling of a covenant people, for sending the prophets, for keeping promises, for the gift of Jesus Christ, including his birth, life, and atoning death and resurrection, and for the particular gifts of the congregation. As Jesus gave thanks on the night he was betrayed, Christians have associated the prayer of thanksgiving with the breaking of bread ever since.

Prayers of Supplication

This form of prayer offers us the chance to be completely honest before God, offering up our concerns and turning to God in order to ask for something from God that we dearly seek. We come before God's presence with the faith that God will hear and answer us, and that the love of God will allow us to ask without fear and to trust in God's grace to grant our requests. Such prayers may be voiced aloud or prayed in silence. When people name their concerns, it is appropriate for the congregation to respond with a refrain such as: "You hear our prayer." There are two forms of supplication: petition and intercession.

Prayers of Petition

Prayers of petition are the most common form of supplication and the most universal. We pray a petition, if only a brief one, when in distress: "God spare me" or "Lord, help me." Whenever we are dealing with a threat to our lives or security, we pray for help quite naturally and almost without thinking about it. "Foxhole prayers" are prayers uttered in a moment of desperation when we realize that our only hope is in God. They are signs that we have come to grips with the supreme fact that God is our only real refuge and strength. Personal prayers of petition can be the most honest form of prayer of all, for in them, we dare to bring to God what we really desire. We don't need to censor them because we can trust God to answer them in God's own wisdom, not necessarily in the way we want or expect.

On the other hand, public prayers of petition must be censored a bit lest we reveal more than we wish about ourselves. We may even want them to be anonymous. In some worship services, petitions are written on slips of paper and then brought forward with the offering plates. They are then woven into a pastoral prayer and names may either be used or left out, depending upon the desires of the petitioner. In public worship, our desires are expressed in a more public way. Our petitions may be expressed jointly as we pray for those things that all of us seek together: peace, strength, wisdom, hope, trust, grace, courage, and faithfulness. Such prayers are also expressed in our hymnody. Hymns of petition include "Jesus, Lover of My Soul" (a prayer for strength), "Breathe on Me, Breath of God" (a prayer for inner peace and certainty), "Guide My Feet" (a prayer for guidance amid the uncertainties of life), "God of Grace and God of Glory" (a prayer for courage to live life faithfully in difficult times). As we sing these hymns, we are seeking the same gifts from God that are otherwise expressed in spoken words.

Prayers of Intercession

The second form of supplication is prayer for others. In the classical order of intercession, the order is as follows: (1) the universal church, that it may be obedient to the Lord in its life and mission; (2) the nation and all in authority, especially the president, Congress, and our state officials; (3) the general welfare of the whole world, for peace on earth, justice and harmony among nations; (4) the concerns of the local community outside of the church, the neighborhood, city, or other communities; (5) those who are in trouble, sickness, grief or any other kind of difficulty. Maintaining this order gives balance to the prayer and provides assurance that the breadth of concerns necessary has been maintained. To leave even one of these concerns out of the prayer is to shortchange the congregation. All of these concerns may be expressed elsewhere in the order of worship and in other forms of prayer or in song.

Very few hymns of intercession exist, but there are a few, such as "O Christ, the Healer," a prayer for spiritual and physical healing; "Where Cross the Crowded Ways of Life" is a prayer of intercession for the problems of urban life; "God, Bless Your Church with Strength!" is a prayer for the faithfulness of the church; "God Bless America" and the last verse of "My Country, 'Tis of Thee" are prayers for the nation; and "Eternal Father, Strong to Save" lifts up prayer for those at sea, especially those in the navy. Most hymns for the church include those present, so they are more petition than intercession.

Intercession concludes with a remembrance of those who have gone before us. The hymn "For All the Saints" should be sung more often than on All Saints' Day and for funerals. A vivid sense of connection with those who have gone on before us will strengthen us for faithfulness.

Prayers of Dedication

We conclude our prayers with those of dedication; as we offer ourselves to God, we submit our lives to God's will. Such action needs to be expressed in every worship service as a response to the Word proclaimed. The presentation and dedication of our lives along with the gifts we bring is one way to express this need.

Hymns frequently express this action more than other forms of prayer. Such hymns as "Here I Am, Lord," "Make Me a Captive, Lord," "O for a Closer Walk with God," "Take My Life," "We Give Thee but Thine Own," "Come, Labor On," and "Lead On, O King Eternal" are good examples of dedication.

A congregation that has a clear sense of the power of prayer will be a congregation that is filled with the power of the Holy Spirit.

Notes

1. *Book of Order,* W-2.1001.
2. *Sing the Faith* (Louisville: Geneva Press, 2002).
3. *Book of Common Worship* (Louisville: Westminster John Knox Press, 1993), 81.

Questions for Discussion and Reflection

1. Do you ever practice silent prayer, or meditation, alone? As a part of worship? What makes this way of prayer challenging?
2. Rice reminds us that most psalms are prayers. Are your prayers as honest or as open with God as many of them are? What might keep you from praying prayers of intense emotion?
3. Which form of prayer (adoration, confession, thanksgiving, supplication) do you use the most in your prayer life? Which one do you pray the least? Why do you think this is? What about your congregation? Is there one form of prayer that seems more dominant than the others?
4. What are some different ways that prayers of petition and intercessory prayer are prayed in your congregation?
5. How might you be more intentional about connecting your prayer life during the week to Sunday worship?
6. What are some of the ways that you offer yourself to God through prayer? Is this a difficult mode of prayer for you?
7. Rice ends the chapter with the words, "A congregation that has a clear sense of the power of prayer will be a congregation that is filled with the power of the Holy Spirit." Why do you think that he says this? What might characterize the power of the Holy Spirit?

4

Worship and the Natural World

All ancient worship among every people around the world had a distinct connection with the natural world. Whether they were Native Americans, European Celts, Africans, or Hindus, preliterate people made no distinction between the material world and the world of spirits. To survive they lived in harmony with the universe and sought to keep the balance between their lives and the rhythms of the world around them. Thus, they developed rituals for waking, making the fire, and all of the ordinary tasks of life. In addition, they developed special elaborate rituals for occasions of great importance, such as preparation for the hunt, for the killing of the prey and distribution of its carcass, for planting and harvesting, for birth and death, for marriage and a new home. Most of these peoples had a distinct sense of the sacredness of all things: that the spirit world was everywhere present in wind, rain, sun, and stars; in plant and animal life; and in their own bodies. Thus they worshiped with dance and the rhythm of drums as well as with words and song. Dance may be the oldest form of worship.

The Hebrew people were no exception to the practices of other ancient peoples. They had an appreciation for the powerful forces of the world around them, which is obvious in the Psalms. Psalm 148 addresses natural elements with the demand that the sun and moon, shining stars, fire and hail, snow and frost, mountains and hills are all to join in praise of God. Psalm 29, which may be the oldest of the Psalms, celebrates God's presence in an approaching storm. The entire psalm is a description of wind and thunder (called "voice of the Lord"), and the lightning and rain are seen as God's agents.

As an agricultural people, the Hebrews were dependent upon the forces of wind and rain for their crops. They also celebrated the arrival of the seasonal rains, which marked the beginning of the new year, the harvesting of grapes at the feast of booths, and the harvest of barley as the origin of the feast of Passover. Even though they developed a strong sense of the transcendence of God, they never lost a sense of God's presence in all things. They prayed when washing before meals, they prayed in gratitude for the harvest, and their spirituality was strongly connected to their agricultural life.

Today we live in a society in which we relegate the presence of God to a spiritual dimension even as we become alienated from the natural world that surrounds us. However, we cannot escape our relationship to the natural world. Our very bodies are part of the earth, and the air we breathe connects us with other living things. In our artificial setting, most of us are quite unaware of our relationship with the natural world. We are artificially cooled in hot weather and warmed when it is cold. We are sheltered from the wind and rain, and only when a natural event of some magnitude takes place, such as a tsunami, hurricane, tornado, volcanic eruption, or severe drought, do we pay attention. Yet, by our careless use of the earth, our poisoning of the air and water, we may be inadvertently making this place unlivable for future generations. Worship can remind us of our connection to the world.

Whenever we worship, we bring all that we are to each occasion. We are flesh and blood people and our bodies are part of what we have to offer to the Lord. We also use physical elements around us because we need them in worship; they are part of our life also. We are not disembodied minds or spirits but creatures who live in the midst of a wonderful creation. The incarnation of Jesus as a human being is expressed in our relationship to the physical world. Although Quakers have worshiped very successfully without the use of many material elements, the rest of Christianity stresses the connection between the spiritual and the physical by appropriating physical elements and bodily movement as part of the act of worship.

Church Buildings

Most of the time, we worship in buildings that are set aside for this unique purpose. Our church buildings proclaim to the community that God is present, and they invite people to pay attention to the spiritual reality. By the very image of the cross, they demonstrate that Christ is among us. Our buildings are signs as well as gathering places. There have been efforts to establish congregations without buildings, often named "churches without walls," but these experiments have rarely succeeded because we need common space that has a sacred connection, surrounds us with symbols of faith, and has the quality of the sacred by its association with prayer and other acts of worship.

The Directory of Worship says this about space: "Christians may worship in any place, for the God who created time also created and ordered space. The Old Testament tells us God met with people in many different places. Yet particular locations became recognized as places where people had special encounter with God, so they arranged space in such a way as to remember and enhance that meeting."[1] Our experience isn't very different. We remember sacred moments and attach them to places that acquire a sense of holiness by the association. How else could one explain the nearly universal resistance to major changes in church buildings? We resist change because of the connections we make. Certain places on the earth have acquired sacredness through centuries of use as places of prayer. The abbeys of Scotland and Ireland were built on sites of pre-Christian Celtic worship. Early settlers in the Americas built churches on sites sacred to the Native peoples who lived there, sometimes without even consciously knowing the connection. Pilgrimages have been made in some places on earth for centuries, and the feet of those who walked that way have left behind a sense of holiness, even when those who follow may not share the faith of those who went before. The City of Jerusalem has acquired holiness for Muslims, Christians, and Jews and because of this is a fiercely contested and divided city.

Common space is important for several reasons. We need neutral space because whenever we meet in someone's home, no matter how gracious the host may be, we are all conscious that we are in another's space, and we are guests there. We need space that is common to us all and to which we are equally attached. Common space that is set apart for worship is a constant reminder of the presence of God. It is true that we often get too attached to our church buildings—but the connection does make sense. The longer we have worshiped in one place, the more memories we associate with that space. We have spent many Christmas Eves there, we have attended baptisms, received Communion, heard sermons and anthems, sung hymns, been part of weddings and funerals. The space has connection with many special occasions in our lives. It has become an important part of who we are, a reminder of important moments, and a source of inspiration.

There is no such thing as a Presbyterian form of church architecture, but there are important clues to how a Presbyterian church building might look according to the Directory for Worship. The Directory says only that the space "should facilitate accessibility and ease of gathering, should generate a sense of community, and should open people to reverence before God."[2] Each of those qualities is easy to put into words but says a lot about the kind of building that serves well to facilitate worship.

First is accessibility, which means more than making sure that architectural barriers such as stairs do not keep some people out. This space must be welcoming to all. Often, in an effort to build grand buildings, we dwarf human beings so that they feel insignificant and lost. Church space should be of human dimensions and should cause people to recognize our own value to God. Thus, it should be welcoming, intimate, with easy access and respect for the limitations of those who may have difficulty seeing, hearing, moving, or understanding. Children, especially, should be respected in the design so that they have space for movement, places where the seating fits their bodies, and symbols that grab their attention and serve as teachers. But even adults with no noticeable disability need to feel that they are comfortably accommodated, that they do not have to peer around posts in order to see the action, and that they can hear clearly and move in and out as the order of service dictates (for example, getting up for Communion, seating late-comers, coming forward to make an announcement, and so forth). Pews spaced too closely together make it difficult for these actions to take place.

Second, community is created when people can see one another and not simply the backs of the heads of those in front of them. Fixed pews have limited purpose in today's world, whereas moveable seating is inexpensive and attractive. Seats can be arranged in a variety of patterns, such as a semicircle or in rows that face one another. The faces of fellow worshipers may be the single most important symbol to represent the gospel, since Christ took the form of one of us, reminding us that we are his friends, and promising to be among us. We are a community. As such, we need to be present to one another, and the space for worship should enhance that sense of being a family.

Part of a welcoming space is comfort. If the pews are uncomfortable, people will not feel welcome no matter what we do. If people cannot hear because the acoustics are poor, they will not feel welcome. Too often we have tried to make the space look inviting by covering it with fabric that deadens the sound. Even new church buildings often absorb sound so that each person feels as though he or she were speaking or singing alone. If the lighting is too harsh or too dim, we will feel shut out. Every worship space should consider the needs of flesh and blood people who must sit there, move about, see, and hear.

The third qualification is reverence, which is a difficult term to define. For some people reverence suggests an atmosphere that is quiet, restful, unspoiled, orderly, traditional, dimly lighted, and of a character that suggests otherness. For others, reverence may imply singing, raising hands, clapping hands, and other actions, violating the first sense of the word. A space that enables worshipers to experience reverence for God must provide for openings through which a sense of the holy may be glimpsed, and that usually means space for some sense of being alone before God. A high ceiling may do that, but the use of color can add to that sense also. A hidden source of light from a window that cannot be seen may speak about the hiddenness of God. A visual sense of what is taking place is most important whether through the presence of visual symbols as reminders or the furnishings that speak of the functions of worship.

Centers for Worship

The three principle centers for worship that need to be emphasized are the pulpit for the reading and proclamation of the Word, the font for assembling for baptisms, and the table for gathering for the meal. Each of these centers has its own needs, and the three should be related in an artistic unity.

The Pulpit

Whatever else can be said about the pulpit, it needs to be located so that people can see the person preaching and, above all, hear what is being said. The less people have to crane their necks, the more they will be able to attend to what is being spoken. Often, in an effort to stress the centrality of preaching, the pulpit is elevated so that the congregation can only see with discomfort because the preacher towers over them. All sense of relationship between preacher and people is difficult to maintain when the architecture creates this separation. This may explain why many preachers today have abandoned the pulpit in order to stand in the center aisle so that they can have eye contact with the people and be part of them as they preach.

An ideal pulpit should be centrally located so all can see, raised enough to enable both visual and aural communication to take place but not so removed as to isolate the preacher. It should hold space for a large pulpit Bible, and if possible, that Bible should be visible so that it is clear that Scripture is central to the preached sermon. In some congregations, a deacon or elder carries the Bible in at the beginning of worship, and this action emphasizes the importance of Scripture.

Even the action of finding a text, turning pages carefully to locate a chapter, is a testimony to the location of that verse in the whole of Scripture. A marker will help the preacher to avoid the embarrassment of vainly searching for the day's text!

The Font

The font should be large enough to take some prominence in the worship space. It should be located either at the rear so that people pass by on their way in and out of the sanctuary, or in the front for all to see from their pews and be reminded of their own baptism. Many fonts are so small that they bear no witness to the fact that this sacrament is practiced among us. Rear-placed fonts have the advantage of serving as regular reminders of the grace of our own baptism, but they require that people turn around for baptisms or even, in small congregations, that they get out of their seats and gather around the font. Such movement may be a blessing. The font should be large enough so that it is possible to pour water from a pitcher and hear it splash and to baptize by pouring water from a scoop or shell over the head of the person being baptized. We tend to be so sparing with the water that we do not immerse, pour, or sprinkle but instead merely use a damp finger!

The Table

The Communion table should also be large enough that the space does not dwarf it but not so large that it no longer suggests a table. Many churches built some decades ago have tables that resemble a high altar, constructed like a sarcophagus and pushed against the wall so that the pastor who serves Communion must use it as a kind of sideboard or bring in another table on Communion occasions. In order to serve as a reminder of the importance of the sacrament, the table that is used should be the same one that is regularly seen and perhaps even have on it a pitcher, chalice, and plate. Placing too much besides these on the table detracts from its primary usage and is like using the font as a vase for cut flowers. Whatever we would not put upon our own dining room table at home does not belong on the Lord's Table. A white cloth normally covers the table on Communion occasions and should not reach all the way to the ground so that the legs of the table are obscured.

These furnishings should be well made and beautiful but should not be ornate. Jesus did not use a gold chalice at the Last Supper, and in our efforts to use lovely things we may destroy the simplicity of the occasion. Simple pewter or pottery Communion ware speaks powerfully to the inclusion of all and is a good reminder of Jesus' simple life as a peasant among peasants.

How to place these three major pieces of furniture is a matter of taste for each congregation, but the three should always be in some balance with each other. We most likely use the pulpit more often, so it may be given central place, yet the gatherings that take place at the font and table may require more attention to the need for adequate space for movement.

These three primary furnishings should be well lighted so that even those with some vision impairment can see the actions performed there. Indeed the whole worship space should have adequate light. Our Puritan ancestors preferred the use of clear-glass windows because before electricity they needed all the natural light possible for people to see their hymnals and Bibles. Artificial light should be carefully used today in balance with natural light to enhance areas to be highlighted, always providing enough light for people to find their way to their seats and to see the action clearly.

Symbols

Aside from the furniture already described, the other symbols in the worship space should include hymnals easily located near each seat and bulletins, which are put in the hands of all worshipers and which provide clear directions for following the service with a minimal number of inserts (which easily confuse people).

In the medieval church, the use of stained glass was a primary teaching tool for a society in which nearly all people were illiterate. They could look at the pictures and see the faith story laid out for them. Even highly literate people need visual reminders. We appeal to all of the senses, including that of sight; we either do it well or poorly. Our windows, unless they are clear glass, are a wonderful way to tell our Christian story. In many churches today, banners and paraments that can be changed with the themes of the seasons of the church year are added to the fixed art of the windows.

Our central symbol, the cross, should be used carefully and powerfully. Too often, churches put crosses everywhere and they lose their meaning by indiscriminate use. At least one cross of sufficient size to dominate the worship space should hang on a wall behind the pulpit and table so that it can speak loudly of the faith we celebrate. Our Protestant sensibility about "graven images" has made us reluctant to use sculpture and even somewhat reluctant to use two-dimensional pictures on the walls. However, these and other symbols of the faith—

the fish, the circle, the triangle with a circle inside to represent the Trinity, bunches of grapes and a vine, shocks of wheat, signs of the Holy Spirit such as a descending dove, the ark (symbol of the church), and many others—can be used to beautify the space and to remind us of the faith we hold dear.

The most significant symbols are the three already named: the open Bible, the water of baptism, and the bread and wine of Communion. Each of these symbols needs to be made the most of in size and placement. A large pulpit Bible is far more significant than a small handheld one or pieces of paper with the text typed on them. A large loaf of bread and a pitcher of wine are more representative of the one body in Christ than precut squares and prepoured miniature glasses. The action of breaking and pouring is part of the heart of the action in the Lord's Supper.

The Actions of the People

We use our bodies to worship God and we do this in many ways. We worship by sitting attentively to hear the word spoken, we bow or kneel for prayer, we stand for praise, especially for songs and hymns of praise, we process the gifts of bread and wine into the room, we process the gifts of the people's offerings down the aisle to present them before the congregation to God. We may come forward to receive Communion, at least occasionally, and in the process we pass fellow believers on our way forward and as we return to our pews. The act of breaking off a piece of the bread and dipping it in the cup is something physical. A very few congregations now have kneelers in the pews so that those who wish to pray in this manner may do so. Kneeling is a unique posture for prayer and the posture itself may be an aid for prayer for some. We may hold out our hands so that they form the shape of the cross in order to receive the elements of Communion; we fold our hands for prayer; and we may make the sign of the cross at the conclusion of prayer, receiving the assurance of pardon, or the benediction. We pass the offering plate to one another; we exchange the ritual passing of the peace by shaking hands, or with a hug or even a kiss on the cheek. When we observe pew Communion, we pass the elements to one another, serving each other as equals before the Lord, perhaps saying something such as "the bread of life" or "the cup of the new covenant" to the one we serve. We may join hands following the benediction to symbolize our unity as we sing a response. In many ways we are active with our bodies and thus conscious of our creation as physical beings whose worship is not only spiritual but physical as well.

The setting in which we surround ourselves in worship, the signs we use to represent elements of our faith, the actions we make in worship all speak of an incarnate God whose creatures we are by our creation. Flesh is a good gift from God and we worship best by using all that we are to honor God. Martin Luther once said something like this: We were given five senses by God; if we neglect to use all of them, we are less than grateful. Too often, our worship treats people as if they were ears and minds and little else. We offer precious little to see, almost nothing to touch, and only rarely opportunities to move.

A truly fulfilling worship will appeal to all the senses and treat us as whole people. Our bodies are not incidental, nor do they get in the way of our spiritual lives—they are part of how we grow in God, the God who became incarnate in a human body.

Notes
1. *Book of Order,* W-1.3020.
2. *Book of Order,* W-1.3024.

Questions for Discussion and Reflection

1. Look about you in your place of worship and notice what catches your eye. Does that particular place in the building change from time to time, or is it fixed (like a window)?
2. As you reflect upon worship as you usually experience it, what physical movement is normal in the service? How does movement affect you?
3. Have you ever witnessed a liturgical dance? How did it serve to interpret the gospel to you?
4. How could your church worship space be made more accessible to children, the elderly, people with disabilities?
5. When you are served Holy Communion, do you like to break off a piece of the bread yourself, have it broken for you and handed to you, or precut? Why do you prefer it that way?

Worship and the Occasions of Life

5

Worship is connected to all parts of our life. No event is too unimportant or trivial to offer to God and to seek God's blessing. Rituals have been created through the centuries to help us mark and hallow the most important life events: birth, coming of age, graduation from school, marriage, establishing a new home, sickness, and death. New rituals need to be created to help us to remember and mark other significant events such as divorce, adoption, a new job, retirement, and leaving a congregation because of a move.

Our need to celebrate these events is like that of ancient people all around the world. It is natural to want to make the most of those events that are most important to us. We need to mark them in ways that recognize their importance, help us to remember them, and sacralize them so that they are holy times. Even the antireligious Soviet Union created secular rituals for marriage, birth, and death. The Soviet state recognized the human need for such forms of celebration and tried to fill the void it had created by its effort to destroy the church and establish a communist atheist state.

People who may not otherwise attend worship regularly are often found at a wedding, a baptism, or a funeral. Instead of criticizing those who attend only at such times, it may be important to recognize that such occasions are important means of proclaiming the gospel to those who might not otherwise hear it. We do not take advantage of a captive audience, but we must recognize how important what we say and do at these events is for many who come. People will very likely form their opinion about the church on the basis of what they hear and see, and may even decide to give the church a second try! If they hear a message of condemnation or exclusivism, they may have the worst of their prejudices about Christianity reinforced.

Baptism

Baptisms are important events about which more has been said elsewhere, but we must first acknowledge that every baptism of an infant is a welcome into the world, a means of expressing gratitude for the miraculous gift of a new life, and an appreciation for the uniqueness of each child who becomes part of the congregation and is added to the roll of the baptized members of the church. Parents, grandparents, other family members, sponsors, and friends gather with the members of the congregation for this important ceremony.

Since the sacrament of baptism is a response to the gospel, the order of worship places baptism after the sermon just as it does the sacrament of Holy Communion.

Efforts to move baptism to a spot earlier in the service, often out of a desire to reduce the anxiety of parents who worry about the baby getting fussy, take away the importance of this sacrament as a form of enactment of the Word and tend to reinforce the idea that it is no more than a charming ceremony in which the child is given a name. If a child is fussy, the parents might sit out for an early part of the service in a separate room and then bring the baby in for the baptism itself. Most members of congregations enjoy the sound of a baby, even the cries, because these sounds are reminders of new life and hope for the future of the church.

Baptism clearly represents the free grace of God. It acts out that grace by bestowing the blessing of the Triune God upon a baby who does not understand what is happening, or upon an adult who may believe she or he understands but who is a babe in the faith also with much to learn about the meaning of his or her baptism. Whether in the baptism of a baby or of an adult who has come to faith, baptism is always a response to what God has done previously.

The practice of permitting the parents, in consultation with the session, to choose sponsors who will assist in the Christian training of the child is recognition of the frailty of life. Parents may not always live to see their children reach adulthood, and the mobility of our society means that a family may very likely move to several communities and thus belong to more than one congregation while the children are growing up. These situations make the promises of the present congregation to be responsible for the growth and nurture of that child in the Christian faith somewhat empty. Thus it is that the promises of any single congregation need to be affirmed by people who can follow that child and its parents through the trials of babyhood, childhood, adolescence, and as long as possible until that person is able to make a personal statement of faith. A duty that belongs to everyone may, in fact, end up as no one's responsibility. Sponsors are people who make a commitment to act on behalf of family and congregation to carry out the promises made. They should always be people of faith so that they can join the parents in answering the questions with integrity. The congregation is a corporate sponsor, and when a family moves and transfers its membership, the names of the baptized children are included on the letter of transfer.

Both individual sponsors and the sponsorship of the whole congregation are signs of the reality that no two people have the strength, spiritual fortitude, energy, or intelligence to raise a child alone. All parents need help. Birth is a crisis in a family, and the dynamics of all family members change with the addition of a new child. In the same way, when a person is baptized on the basis of his or her own faith, that person needs support to fulfill the vows made. Living the Christian life requires models of what that means in practical life. It requires the support, encouragement, and prayers of others. We cannot be Christians in isolation. Even hermit monks have a community out of which they live and turn to spiritual guides from that community who meet with them on regular occasions. People who are baptized as adults need sponsors just as much as do little children. Probably every Christian needs a sponsor of some sort, someone who can pray for and encourage each person and help to sort out life options, make crucial decisions, and stay faithful in the midst of temptation.

Rituals of Childhood

As children are raised in the context of the congregation's life, there are rituals that mark their progress toward a mature faith. They may be enrolled in what is often called the cradle roll, with their names kept before the congregation as reminders of who they are. As they grow and take part in Sunday church school, they are prepared for and welcomed at the Lord's Table as they receive instructions in the meaning of this sacrament. They need to be included in the educational program of the church. They receive a Bible of their own at some point, often as they enter fourth grade. They take part in projects that help them to recognize the importance of service. Mission trips for teens are a wonderful way to build a sense of community and learn about other people whose lives may be enriched by the work that the group performs. Such work experiences also help adolescents to express some of their idealism. Teens are also included in a class to prepare them for active membership. This class is often taught by the pastor and marks the first occasion for them to receive full attention from the pastor, who is the pastor of the children and youth as much as of the adults.

This class, often called the confirmation class or commissioning class, meets for a period of time, sometimes for a year or longer. During that time, the participants are taught the meaning of the faith, focusing especially on the questions that will be asked of them later by the session. They need to know, above all, what it means to confess Jesus as their Lord and Savior and the implications of that affirmation for the rest of their lives. They may also be instructed in Presbyterian history, government, and worship so that they appreciate the context in which they will live out their commitment. The questions asked of them, however, do not focus supremely upon Presbyterian distinctives but upon the faith of the church universal. If the Apostles' Creed is ever used in worship, it should be used on two occasions: baptism and reception of new members. People are not baptized as Presbyterians but as Christians, and we do not use the family name because at least for that moment in time, their last name is "Christian." When they make their personal confession of faith, they are also confessing their faith, not in a particular denomination, but as Christians who share a common faith with millions of other people.

Too often, the young people see the class as leading to a kind of graduation from the special classes they have attended, and after its conclusion they are no longer seen around the church. Such a misunderstanding of membership commitment is a serious issue, and we need to do everything we can to make sure that young people realize how their confession connects them with others and how the adventure of being a Christian lasts a lifetime.

The decision to become a confessing Christian requires as much ceremony as necessary to mark the occasion as sacred and special. Because our society has no ritual for moving from childhood to adulthood other than receiving a driver's license, the ceremony of uniting with the church may become a "coming of age" ritual, like a bar or bat mitzvah for Jews. To make the most of this occasion, we must invest the ceremony with as much dignity, solemnity, joy, and appreciation as possible. The young people may wear robes for the occasion and be presented with flowers, Bibles, certificates of membership, crosses, or other symbols appropriate to the day. The pastor and elders and perhaps family members or sponsors may make these presentations to signify the unity of the biological family with the church family. Holding a reception for them after worship is one more way to help them to feel that they matter.

Leaving Home

Leaving home is a special moment for most young people, whether that means joining the military, going off to college, or simply moving out of the family home to take a job elsewhere. The separation from loved ones that leaving home requires is both natural and healthy and, at the same time, somewhat painful for all the parties involved. The parents grieve the empty room left behind, and the young person may be excited by the new adventures. However, he or she is very likely to experience homesickness as well.

The church needs to develop some ritual way of helping families deal with this crisis. We are better at celebrating graduation from high school than the consequences that event brings with it. It is good to have graduates honored in a service of worship, but it is also good to recognize those who move on to new lives. Some ritual of commissioning of those who leave for the military, college, or a new job should be developed by the session. This ritual would include laying on of hands and prayer, followed perhaps by a reception in their honor. Such a commissioning is important enough to do for one individual, but it may be planned to include all of those whose leave-taking is occurring at about the same time. We must be very careful not to put all the emphasis upon those who are going off to college or we demonstrate elitism.

Marriage

Marriage today is in considerable trouble. A great many marriages end up in divorce. Most experts say that nearly one out of every two marriages ends in failure; and even if there are no children involved, the sense of hurt, betrayal, failure, guilt, loneliness, and anger may persist for years for one or both of the two parties. The United Church of Christ in its *Book of Worship* has an excellent service for the recognition of a divorce, which might be used as part of a worship service but more likely will be performed with part of the family and close friends. This service is both a time for confession of failure and a time for forgiveness and welcome to new life achieved by letting go of the past.

Even though we admit the difficulties that marriage brings, every marriage is also a time for celebration and hope. Pastors may refuse to perform marriages if they are convinced that Christian commitment or readiness for taking on the duties of the new relationship are lacking. It is often true, however, that the most promising of marriages end in divorce and the one no one expected to last endures. There is no predicting human behavior because we are free agents, and only God knows our futures.

Christian marriage is a ceremony of the church, not just of the two people who come to be married. They will have their own ideas about what they want in the service, but the pastor must be the judge of what is appropriate. The vows, which are intended to be lifelong, should be taken even though we recognize the possibility of failure. At least at the beginning, we should expect the best for the two people, bless their relationship, and honor their commitments to each other. As we surround them with our love, we assure them that they are not alone as they face new trials and opportunities in their life together. This is true even if previously they have been living together. More often than might be expected, marriage drastically alters a relationship. Marriage does something important to the relationship that is both frightening and empowering. Because marriage is a public event, the ceremony also involves family members and friends who promise to honor the new relationship and support the couple.

The vows of the couple are the heart of the service and should be spoken aloud so that all may hear. The minister is simply present to witness those vows, so the couple should be encouraged to memorize their vows, if possible, and speak them to one another. Above all, the wedding ceremony should be a time of great joy and celebration. The pastor should be comfortable as leader so that clear directions can be given to the participants and they can be put at ease.

The pastor may employ the assistance of a wedding coordinator who can handle details such as flowers, picture-taking, questions about seating, and even the lineup for the processional. No pastor can be in two places at once.

Moving into a New Home

Whether or not the home is a new one, every move is a new opportunity and needs the help of God. Blessing a new home is a lovely way to give those who are moving a sense of the sacred in their own living space. A small group of friends, church members and officers, and the pastor gather in the living room or just outside the main door and go from room to room, asking for God's blessing on the activities of the household. Incense could also be used to create a sense of the sacred in each room. Such a ritual is included in the *Book of Occasional Services*, which has been produced to accompany the *Book of Common Worship*.

A similar ceremony might also be used for saying good-bye to a home that has been lived in for a long time—for example, when a person or couple is moving into a retirement community. Saying good-bye to space that has been hallowed by years of living is not easy and may be very traumatic. A service of thanksgiving for the blessings of life that have been experienced in that space is a wonderful way to say goodbye, even though it is likely to provoke tears of honest feelings.

Commissioning to New Work

We already have services of this kind but they could be applied to almost any new form of service or employment. Because in our Reformed heritage we understand all work to be a divine calling, we appreciate the fact that people are called to other work than that of ordained ministry. They may be called to public service, teaching, social work, medical work, or other forms of service to others that need recognition by the church. We pray for them, give thanks to God for their dedication, and send them out with our blessing. Our Presbyterian resource *Book of Occasional Services* contains such a service, appropriately named a Service of Commissioning to Ministry Outside the Congregation. The introduction to the services makes it clear that this service can be used to commission people for a variety of ministries: mission volunteers, community volunteers, chaplains, representatives to church conferences, and so forth.[1] The importance of this service is the recognition that ministry is not the province of ordained ministers only but belongs to all the people of God. The problem with this service may be its limitation to callings related to the church. In fact, people may be called to serve on a town council or school board or in another civic role, and that calling is just as much service to God or ministry as callings within the institutional church.

Leaving a Congregation

When a person moves from a congregation, some recognition of past service needs to be included in worship. *The Book of Occasional Services* includes such a service, which is very brief and can be part of any Sunday worship service. Such recognition is an important way to admit the pain, or at least ambiguity, of leaving a community that has been supportive and a place to grow in faith. Even though the person may be looking forward to a new life in a different place, the excitement is muted by the sadness in leaving behind the familiar. Such a service is also a good way to acknowledge the gifts that have been shared by that person in various forms of service.

Sickness

When sickness comes upon us, we know our weakness and helplessness. In spite of the best of modern medicine, our bodies wear out, catch diseases that seem to defy the best of preventative care, and cause us great distress and pain. At such times we realize that we are not in charge of our destiny, and that realization of our helplessness isn't a pleasant fact. In our modern world, we have been led to believe that we can all live long and happy lives by taking good care of ourselves, eating properly, exercising regularly, taking vitamins, and receiving good medical care. But even these precautions cannot protect us from sickness: cancer can strike almost out of the blue, or a diagnosis of Alzheimer's comes as a total shock. We cannot insure ourselves from misfortune and sickness.

From the beginning, the church has recognized the importance of ministries of healing. Jesus set the pattern with his ministry of teaching, preaching, and healing, and the early church engaged in a healing ministry in his name. James gives instructions to those who are sick to send for the elders of the church to pray and lay hands upon them.

Many diseases seem to defy all our best efforts to heal through scientific medicine. AIDS, multiple sclerosis, ALS, many forms of mental illness, Alzheimer's disease, brain tumors and other forms of cancer, diabetes, and other diseases seem just as devastating now as they were decades ago for those who suffer and those who must stand by and watch them. We do not understand why disease strikes some people and not others. Even cancer seems to attack some who live in the same community and are subject to the same environmental hazards as others who are spared. Not every smoker develops lung cancer. The mystery of disease is at the core of our life and the question "Why me?" seems impossible to answer. Our best efforts are not very helpful even though well intended: "God knows what is best," "God has a plan for you but we just don't see it now," "We just have to trust that God will bring good out of this situation." Sometimes all our answers do is make the suffering more difficult.

A ministry of healing is being revived in the church today. Because we are less enamored by the promises of science, we are also more open to the possibility of spiritual healing that cannot be accounted for by any means other than miracle. We know from several trustworthy research projects that people who pray are, on the whole, more likely to recover from illness. There is a connection between sickness and faith that defies rationality. There are times when the laying on of hands with prayer is an occasion for a miracle of healing to take place. But even when healing does not take place, the ministry of prayer can make a difference in the way we handle illness, our attitude of defeat or victory, depression or radiant joy. Our attitude has a great deal to do with our faith, and faith can be fortified by the ministry of spiritual healing.

Whether in the midst of a worshiping congregation, at home, or in the hospital, the pastor, elders, and Christian friends can gather to pray and lay hands on the sick person. Their loving concern, faith, and prayer are strong medicine. These may be supplemented with the use of the oil of healing and the sign of the cross. *The Book of Common Worship* contains services for healing with a congregation or for individuals, and both have their place. Sometimes the whole congregation may be invited to come to a special service of healing, and as they feel called to respond, individuals may come forward for the laying on of hands. The corporate nature of such services adds to their power. There are also many other times when the sick person is not able to come to the church and the church must go to that person instead.

Reconciliation

Even though the Protestant reformers rejected the sacrament of penance, they recognized the importance of a ritual of forgiveness. There are times when the corporate prayer of confession is sufficient, but there are other times when guilt or a rupture in relationships requires a more personal and direct ritual. John Calvin believed that a chief function of the elders was to hear the confessions of the people. Certainly it is true that pastors are often sought out for counseling by people when, in fact, more than good psychological direction is needed; they need some assurance that God has not rejected them, some sign of their forgiveness, which can only be offered by someone who has heard the worst they can tell about themselves.

People often carry around a sense of terrible guilt for years, which drags them down, keeps them from moving ahead with their lives, and ultimately becomes self-defeating. Until they can experience some sense of relief, they cannot grow in wholeness. The rituals of reconciliation with God are wonderful tools for caregivers and spiritual leaders to help them. These rituals are included in nearly all books of worship of different denominations. Roman Catholics have moved to a broader understanding of their ritual of penance and have captured the essence of its newer meaning with a new name, "the ritual of reconciliation." At the same time, we Protestants have moved to accept what our forebearers knew about the human psyche, that we have difficulty accepting the mercy of God. The good news is too good to be believable, so too often we carry our guilt with us. Prayer, the sign of the cross, and anointing with oil are tools for bringing relief to the suffering of unrelieved guilt.

Another form of reconciliation can take place when two or more people have become alienated from one another and a third party brings them together to admit their mutual need for forgiveness and to ask for the pardon each needs to hear from the other. Such reconciliation might save many marriages and spare congregations from endless struggles for power between factions. In our better moments, we all know that we are flawed and at least partly responsible for the problems we have with each other. No quarrel is ever just one party's fault. The ministry of worship can have a positive effect on broken human relationships.

Death

The greatest of all mysteries is the mystery of death. Because we fear our own death, we also fear those who are dying, shutting them away so we do not have to be disturbed by thoughts of our own mortality. There is a beautiful service for those who are approaching death in our *Book of Common Worship*. This service involves prayers for healing but also prayers for the recognition that a form of healing is release from suffering and welcome into the loving arms of the One who meets us on the other side of death. If the family can gather for such a service, healing of grief may come more quickly, and the person who is dying may, if conscious, be able to die with more assurance, peace, and dignity.

The Witness to the Resurrection is a wonderful chance to summarize the meaning of the life of the one who has died. A sermon on the meaning of life, death, and resurrection may be augmented by close friends who pay special tribute to those qualities of the loved one that have touched them. Every life has had its moments of grace and these moments need to be lifted up.

Today, many people are cremated, and the memorial service is held some time later than the time of death. This delay allows people to travel great distances to be present. The family may scatter or bury ashes at a later time, and the memorial service occurs when the family can participate more fully than if they were preoccupied with a graveside service. Even in those cases in which a graveside service is to take place, it might happen before the public memorial, allowing the close family members and close friends to have a time to grieve by themselves.

In summary, each of life's special occasions is a time to celebrate with worship.

Note
1. Office of Theology and Worship, *Book of Occasional Services* (Louisville: Geneva Press, 1999), 129.

Questions for Discussion and Reflection

1. Have you ever been part of a service of blessing a new home? If not, would you like to have such a service in your home? What difference might it make?
2. Have you ever been part of a service of healing? What was the experience like?
3. What is your understanding of the way the sacraments seal the Word?
4. How often does your congregation celebrate the ministry of the whole people of God in the world?
5. Think about weddings you have attended. How were they services of worship for you?
6. What is the difference between a funeral and a memorial? Do you think that a service without the body present is less painful? Why or why not?

The Ordering of Worship

6

Presbyterian congregations are not free to worship however they may wish, contrary to popular opinion. We are given specific guidance and some clear-cut limitations on the ordering of worship in that part of our Constitution that is called the *Book of Order*. The Directory for Worship is one of three parts of that *Book of Order*, and it has been around in some form since the Westminster Assembly of Divines, which was called by the British Parliament in 1643 for the purpose of setting out the theology, government, and liturgy of the Church of England. Although it has been revised and brought up to date several times since its first writing, the Directory is a unique document among various denominations. It does not provide the wording for particular services but instead provides guidance and some rules for those who plan worship. Someone has said that we are the only denomination that has a book containing only the rubrics for worship.

Our *Book of Common Worship* contains specific orders of worship rather like a prayer book in liturgical traditions, but it is only recommended for use by congregations and has no constitutional force as the Directory does. The Directory only sets forth some basic standards, constitutional limitations or regulations that are binding upon sessions. Thus, each congregation is free to order worship in a way that is congenial to its life and understanding, but it is limited in the exercise of that freedom by the constitutional standards. Such compromise gives Presbyterian congregations the opportunity to design worship that reflects the cultural context of the people. Unlike the liturgical denominations with a mandatory order of worship usually found in a book of worship, and the free churches, which have no limitations, Presbyterians have both freedom and limitations. In order to appreciate and understand our uniqueness, we have to understand our Directory for Worship.

The History of the Directory for Worship

The Directory was a happy compromise for people in Great Britain who were resistant to having a mandatory *Book of Common Prayer* forced upon them by the crown. Scottish Presbyterians and English Puritans were engaged in a struggle for their religious freedom. One of the ways in which the crown sought to control the population was to unite it in a single church with a common pattern of worship. The *Book of Common Prayer* of the Church of England became the tool for that effort and the symbol of all that uniformity meant. To resist the prayer book was a sign of one's allegiance to a higher authority than the crown. Even though the Scots had earlier adopted John Knox's *Form of Prayers,* they came to reject even their own book because it looked too much like the prayer book they rejected. The reaction against the *Book of Common Prayer* grew to become a reaction against all printed, uniform forms of worship and especially against any written prayers. The extremists among the Puritans believed that the only prayers that were genuine and acceptable to God were spontaneous prayers of the heart. Some even rejected repeating the Lord's Prayer on the grounds that it had become a rote repetition and not a heartfelt expression of faith.

When the Puritans and their Scottish allies were victorious and toppled the monarchy of England, the new parliament established a special assembly of religious leaders. That assembly, meeting in Westminster Abbey, drew up the documents that are still enshrined in our Constitution. These documents were designed for the newly reformed church, which they intended to be for all of Great Britain. In the course of its many meetings over a period of several years, the assembly drafted a number of documents that have become central to the Presbyterian tradition: the Westminster Confession of Faith and the Larger and Shorter Catechisms, the Form of Government, the Rules of Discipline, and the Directory for Worship.

Unfortunately, by the time their work was done, the reign of Puritanism was over. After the Lord Protector Oliver Cromwell died, his son Richard was no match for the job. Chaos and confusion broke out. In its concern about lawlessness and disorder, Parliament restored the monarchy. The Church of England was also restored to its previous place as the state church of England, and the work of the Westminster Assembly was adopted only by the Church of Scotland.

The Directory for Worship was a compromise document. There were some who wanted no required forms of worship at all—nothing to interfere with the work of the Holy Spirit. Others, especially the

Scots, wanted order and some limited uniformity and had no objection to certain read prayers, especially during the celebration of the sacraments, which they wanted to protect from distortion or abuse. They wanted freedom from the dictates of the Church of England, yet at the same time they did not want to emulate the free churches, which had no standards except the vote of a congregation. The Directory has served the Presbyterian Church well throughout the ensuing centuries, and it still operates in the same way to inspire freedom and creative imagination among pastors and sessions. At the same time, it holds them to limits, preventing excesses or practices that are out of keeping with our theological tradition, such as the rebaptizing of those who have been baptized previously. The requirement for only one baptism is intended to make it clear that baptism is an act of God whereby the person is included in the covenant community rather than an act of human will or intention.

The History of the *Book of Common Worship*

In spite of our resistance to any set form for worship, we American Presbyterians have produced several editions of an official worship book. In Scotland this book is called the *Book of Common Order of the Church of Scotland.* In late nineteenth-century America, especially among urban and middle-class congregations and pastors, there was a desire for more ordered services. Less ardor and more order was sought because order seemed to be appropriate to Presbyterians' newly acquired social class. As cultured folk we wanted our worship to be an expression of our good taste. Various pastors began to put together service books for use by their own congregations, and the demand for such resources increased so that even the denominational publishing houses began to publish these works. In 1894 the General Assembly of the PCUS adopted a Directory for Worship, which was modified to include liturgical formulas with an appendix that contained actual orders for weddings and funerals.

In 1903 the General Assembly of the PCUSA approved overtures calling for the preparation of a service book and set up a special committee under the leadership of the Reverend Henry van Dyke, pastor of Brick Church, New York. He is still known to us as the author of *The Other Wise Man* and the hymn "Joyful, Joyful, We Adore Thee." The committee reported back to the Assembly of 1906. This was one of those rare monumental assemblies that achieved lasting changes. It approved the first amendments to the Westminster Confession of Faith, modifying it to moderate the severity of the doctrine of predestination and to allow for some human freedom. This assembly also supported the separation of church and state, and it welcomed the reunion with the majority of the Cumberland Presbyterian Church. These two actions detracted somewhat from the importance of another major achievement, the presentation of a service book. As it was, there was considerable debate about whether the church should adopt it. The words of van Dyke to the assembly give a picture of the opposition. He defended the service book by insisting that it was the work of a duly elected committee. He tried to be clear that the work was not a liturgy and did not contain "canned prayers," answering the objection to read prayers. At the same time, he acknowledged that it contained great, live prayers of our forefathers. In the end, the assembly approved the First American Presbyterian *Book of Common Worship* for voluntary use. That action has remained our pattern; since that assembly it has never been mandatory for congregations.

This first *Book of Common Worship* contained orders for morning and evening worship for the Lord's Day and orders for the celebration of Communion, baptism for both adults and children, and confirmation. These services were printed out, including the prayers. A treasury of prayers from the ages and a Psalter selection for responsive readings were included. The book also contained some ancient hymns and canticles. It was a milestone achievement, meant to last well into the new century.

In 1928 when the Episcopal Church produced a new *Book of Common Prayer,* there were calls for the revision of the *Book of Common Worship.* Minor revisions were made and the book was approved in 1932. This edition included texts for various festival days and seasons and the beginning of a lectionary. At this time the PCUS also adopted the book for its own use. This revision coincided with the publication of *The Hymnal* in 1933.

A more complete revision was made by another committee under the leadership of Dr. Hugh Thompson Kerr, author of the hymn "God of Our Life, through all the Circling Years." This 1946 edition showed great influence from the Episcopal worship book. It was written in elegant English and reproduced many of the same prayers as the earlier book. It provided orders for morning prayer (one for each Sunday of the month) and orders for evening worship, also like the Episcopal prayer book. Its rituals for the sacraments were revised so as to resemble the Episcopal services. It adopted a full two-year lectionary from the Church of Scotland, which had been produced only two years earlier in 1944. In addition, it contained a treasury of prayers from the tradition of the church universal. Although this book never made it to the pews of many congregations, it was a useful book for pastors, who used it for sacramental occasions, as well as for marriages and funerals, reception of new members, dedication of memorials, and the ordination of elders and deacons.

In 1955, after only nine years, a new committee was appointed to revise this book. Two weaknesses had been noted: its lack of contemporary awareness and its lack of coherence with the most recent revision of the Directory. It was noted by some critics that the Presbyterians lived with a Puritan directory and an Episcopal prayer book. The committee was asked to produce a book that would be in closer conformity with the work of Calvin and Knox. That same year the PCUSA, the PCUS, the Reformed Church in America, and the Cumberland Presbyterians all adopted a new hymnal, *The Hymnbook*. Unlike its predecessor, this book made concessions to gospel hymns and contained some American hymns, including African American spirituals.

In 1961, under the leadership of Dr. Robert McAfee Brown, the UPCUSA assembly adopted a new Directory for Worship, which was a significantly altered document to reflect the concerns expressed by the General Assembly. In 1970 the Assembly approved *The Worshipbook*, which had been produced by a committee chaired by David Buttrick, pastor of Brick Church, New York. In 1972 *The Worshipbook: Services and Hymns* was published. This publication was unique in its structure, combining both a hymnal and a service book in one single resource so that it could be placed in the pews and used by congregations. The hymns were put in alphabetical order (an unusual feature). This alphabetical ordering made it difficult to locate certain hymns, especially since the first lines were altered in some cases to reflect contemporary English. On the other hand, this ordering freed some hymns from limitation to certain seasons and holidays and other special events, such as funerals, so that they could be sung on other occasions. Perhaps its greatest weakness was that it contained too few hymns to provide an adequate selection and required supplementation by another hymnal. It also failed to use inclusive language; its publication came just before the concern for language that was truly gender inclusive had been seriously considered.

Perhaps the most revolutionary feature of this book was its use of contemporary English. It made a break with Elizabethan English, which—given the fact that the Revised Standard Version of the Bible had been published in 1949—was appropriate. Until then, every part of a Protestant worship service was in Elizabethan English except the sermon and announcements. *The Worshipbook* sought to create a new and appropriate style for contemporary English suitable for worship. Its language was direct and forceful, almost shockingly so, but as we read it today it sounds rather dated, almost as if the Vietnam War were still in progress. This weakness is also a sign of its strength, for it was culturally sensitive to the times.

Liturgically, the most important feature of this book was that the regular order for the Lord's Day was sacramental, holding word and sacrament together following the pattern Calvin vainly tried to get adopted in sixteenth-century Geneva. Until now, all Presbyterian books of worship had a separate order of service for the celebration of the Lord's Supper and for regular preaching services, assuming a divide between the two. *The Worshipbook* also included a new weekly lectionary, which was adapted from the new post-Vatican II Roman Catholic lectionary. It lacked a Psalter because there was confusion as to whose responsibility that was. The subcommittee charged with the hymns did not believe they needed to include a Psalter but the other subcommittee believed otherwise. One wonders today how these two groups could be so disconnected, although the politics of such committees makes it believable. The most serious block to acceptance of this wonderful resource, however, was historical irony. Just as it had begun to use contemporary English, its use of masculine, exclusive language became obvious, and as early as 1974 five different overtures were adopted by presbyteries across the UPCUSA calling for revision of the book to make it language inclusive.

Instead of having a mandatory worship order, this edition followed Presbyterian custom in that it was available voluntarily for congregational use and could be followed to the letter by some and completely ignored by others. Presbyterian worship is thus widely varied, from congregations that use the book and follow it carefully to those who do not even know of its existence. As one visits various congregations, one witnesses everything from a service much like the Episcopal service of Morning Prayer to that of a Pentecostal revival meeting.

It is difficult to determine what makes a service of worship Presbyterian, but some common characteristics can be identified in most congregations. First, the Bible occupies a central place in our worship, whether it is read from a splendid lectern on a raised platform in the chancel area or from within the congregation by a lay reader. There is a sense of hushed attention when the Scripture is read. People know that something important to our faith is taking place. Scripture is reverenced among us, and no worship can be said to take place without some reading from the Bible.

Second, the sermon is also a characteristic common to Presbyterian worship. We require our pastors to preach a "candidating sermon" before a pastor nominating committee or the presbytery of care before being presented to the congregation, and we require that the candidate preach to the congregation, even if the position is for a pastor of education, youth ministry, or pastoral care. We know instinctively that the sermon is a measure of this new pastor's theological compatibility with us and ability to serve us.

Third, the Presbyterian order of worship provides many opportunities for the people to respond and participate through prayer, spoken, silent, and sung. The people may also recite a statement of faith and participate in other ways, such as reading responsively from Scripture.

Fourth, Presbyterian worship always includes concern for others, whether through the offering of our gifts, a minute for mission read from some resource, or spontaneous expressions of concern for the wider world. We know that it is not enough to worship by ourselves. We are part of the wider human family, and we are responsible to God for the way we use our gifts for the greater good.

For a long time it could be said that Presbyterian worship was simple, without unnecessary frills either in the setting or in the structure and language. As we have grown more prosperous and more ecumenical, however, many of our buildings have become more ornate, and even our service structure has become more filled with symbolism and ritual. Such a change in our tradition is part of our adaptation to the modern world, filled with symbols.

The church had other major business concerns during the years after the decade of the approval of the new hymnal, chief among them the issue of Presbyterian reunion and restructure to deal with declining resources. In 1989 the reunited PC(USA) began the process of producing a new service book. Prior to reunion, the United Presbyterian Church (USA) General Assembly had approved an overture calling for the new service book. The effort was quickly joined by the Presbyterian Church U.S. and the Cumberland Presbyterian Church. The work was done through a Joint Office of Worship, which enabled the churches to work together before, during, and after reunion. Harold Daniels was the principal staff person in charge of the project. The reunited Assembly adopted a pieced-together Directory as a temporary measure; it was very unsatisfactory and the process of writing a new one was begun at once. A new Directory was approved in 1989 that reflected contemporary ecumenical scholarship and practice. As early as 1984, the first Supplemental Liturgical Resource was produced for trial use, *The Service for the Lord's Day*. It was followed by six more volumes, all in paperback. Several congregations were invited to participate in a process of dialogue by using these resources, and the various responses were taken into account when the service book was put together in its final form

In 1990 *The Presbyterian Hymnal* was published. Its appearance meant that a hymnal and a service book would be two separate volumes. The argument was made that such a combined book would be far too large to handle. Yet, both the United Methodist Church and the Lutheran Church had proved otherwise—their books contained both the liturgy and the hymns. The failure to produce both elements in one volume meant that the future *Book of Common Worship* would, for the most part, remain a manual for pastors only. Most congregations are not willing to pay the price for two major books in their pews, nor do the pew racks have room to hold both. If congregations have the funds and space for two books, they are likely to purchase hymnals of various types. The new hymnal, produced by a committee chaired by Dr. Melva Costen, is a great achievement in its ability to include hymns of many types, especially a sung Psalter, and also hymns of contemporary origin and standards from many different faith traditions. This hymnal is becoming more and more common among our congregations.

Because the people have limited access to the *Book of Common Worship,* congregations and pastors need to be careful to acknowledge the source of materials used from it whenever they are used in a bulletin by using a simple phrase provided by the book itself: "Reprinted by permission from *Book of Common Worship,* © 1993 Westminster/John Knox Press."

To make its sheer bulk less of a burden for users, two small partial editions have been produced, one of which contains the material from "Daily Prayer" and the "Psalter" and is available for individuals in their own daily devotional lives. The other is an edition of "Pastoral Services," which is useful to pastors for weddings, funerals, and other occasions when the large book is not useable. The size of the *Book of Common Worship* is a major handicap to its use; much that is included does not need to be there, since a book for common worship is a book for the people, not just the pastors. It would have been easy to reduce the bulk by eliminating and placing in another worship book those sections dealing with baptism and those parts for use in pastoral counseling. Marriage services and other pastoral liturgies could also have been omitted.

Besides its size, the *Book of Common Worship* has other features that set it apart from its predecessors. Like *The Worshipbook,* its structure makes it clear that the Service for the Lord's Day is a service of both Word and sacrament and thus seeks to respond to the historic divorce between these two elements in spite of our theology and history. The book also complies with the Directory in setting out an order for worship:

1. gathering around the Word
2. proclaiming the Word
3. responding to the Word
4. the sealing of the Word
5. bearing and following the Word into the world.[1]

Since the "sealing of the Word" means celebrating the sacraments, the combination of Word and sacrament is a normal form of the Lord's Day celebration.

The *Book of Common Worship* contains a number of variations of the Great Prayer of Thanksgiving, or the Prayer of Consecration as it is often called—ten for ordinary time plus sixteen for various days and seasons of the church year and three more for pastoral services, such as weddings and funerals. It also contains eight sets of prayers of the people, which include both bidding prayers and litanies.

One of the finest features of the book is a liturgical Psalter, which is designed for responsive reading or for the use of an antiphon by the people to be repeated after each section is read by the leader. It is also pointed for singing, and psalm tunes are included. This Psalter includes all the psalms used in the Common Lectionary. The translation was borrowed from the Benedictine Order and is wonderfully gender inclusive without spoiling the poetry. After each psalm, a psalm prayer follows, which sums up the psalm's major theme and puts the meaning in Christian terms, rather like the traditional Scottish pattern. These prayers are a better way of presenting the Psalms for Christians than the ancient form of appending a form of the Trinitarian "Gloria" after the last verse.

The *Book of Common Worship* may be accused of being overly ritualistic and wordy. However, it seeks to be ecumenical while at the same time being faithful to our Presbyterian theology and history. That is not an easy balance to maintain; at times it leans toward an Anglican or Roman point of view, as in the inclusion of the monastic hours as the pattern for Daily Prayer instead of our traditional practice of morning and evening prayer for families. Nevertheless, it is a truly Reformed document in the following ways:

1. It has an objective character that focuses upon God and not on the people or their subjective feelings.

2. It combines Word and sacrament, as Calvin wished to do.
3. It restores the use of the Psalms for singing, reading, and prayer.
4. It connects worship with mission.
5. It allows for creative freedom by giving permission throughout for variations.

Every Presbyterian congregation will find its worship life greatly enhanced by using the *Book of Common Worship* as a major resource for worship. It does not have to be followed slavishly but the strengths can be adapted for use. Its use alongside *The Presbyterian Hymnal* provides excellent balance. The *Hymnal* is more contemporary and has been supplemented by a smaller volume, *Sing the Faith,* which contains a wide variety of music from praise songs to music from the Taizé and Iona traditions. It is an excellent complementary volume and has the further asset of being small and inexpensive.

Ordering the Service

The basic pattern laid down in the Directory and fleshed out in the *Book of Common Worship* sets a normative pattern for all Presbyterians. Briefly, our worship should be guided by the following order:

Gathering

We gather in various ways depending upon local custom, but the important thing is that we assemble in a way that creates some distance from our busy lives, provides a chance for us to become a community, and establishes our center in the Lord. All that we do during the gathering moments, whether greeting friends, sitting quietly during the playing of the prelude, or even gathering in silence, should help us to achieve these goals. We need to be ready to encounter the living Lord as a family.

Proclamation of the Word

We hear the Word proclaimed in order to be made new, to meet God, to receive clarity about out lives, and to find guidance for the way we live in a confusing world. All that transpires during this time of worship centers on Scripture: read, sung, and preached.

Responding to the Word

We cannot hear without some response on our part, such as prayer, offering of ourselves and our gifts, statements of faith, or even periods of silent reflection upon what we have just heard. In many ways, this time is the heart of our worship.

Sealing the Word

This is really another form of response in which we receive the sacraments. These ancient rituals act to bind the Word upon our hearts, enacting the meaning of the Word, and they enable us to hear in a different way what has been spoken, this time through actions and concrete objects, which become bearers of the holy to us (water, bread, and wine).

Bearing and Following the Word into the World

At this point our worship helps us to focus our attention upon our lives. We pray for the world and make connection with what we must do to be faithful as Christians in God's world.

These five elements shape all that we do in worship. To omit any of them is to have a truncated experience lacking something of the fullness of the gospel. To put them in a different order may lead to confusion.

Duties of the Pastor and the Session

No Presbyterian congregation will use all of the worship resources now available. However we decide to use or ignore these, we are not free to ignore the Directory. Every session is charged with the responsibility "to provide for the worship of the people of God, including the preaching of the Word, the sharing of the Sacraments, and for the music program, in keeping with the principles in the Directory for Worship"[2]

It is the role of the session to approve those who come to be baptized and to keep an accurate role of baptized members, both infants and adults.[3] The session also determines the frequency of Holy Communion and the manner in which it is served.

The Directory for Worship is very explicit about the responsibilities of the session:

The session shall make provision for the regular

a. preaching of the Word,

b. celebration of the Sacraments,

c. corporate prayer, and

d. offering of praise to God in song.

The session has authority

> e. to oversee and approve all public worship in the life of the particular church with the exception of those responsibilities delegated to the pastor alone

> f. to determine occasions, days, times, and places for worship.

It is responsible

> g. for the space where worship is conducted, including its arrangements and furnishing,

> h. for the use of special appointments such as flowers, candles, banners, paraments, and other objects of art,

> i. for the overall program of music and other arts in the church,

> j. for those who lead worship through music, drama, dance and other arts.[4]

The pastor is responsible for some very specific matters: studying, teaching, and preaching the Word, administering baptism and the Lord's Supper, praying with and for the congregation. With the elders, the pastor is to encourage the people in the worship and service of God, to equip and enable them for their tasks within the church and their mission in the world. Such work is clearly defined and limited. Elsewhere in the Directory, the following duties are enumerated:

> The minister as pastor has certain responsibilities which are not subject to the authority of the session. In a particular service of worship the pastor is responsible for

> > 1. the selection of Scripture and lessons to be read,

> > 2. the preparation and preaching of the sermon or exposition of the Word,

> > 3. the prayers offered on behalf of the people and those prepared for the use of the people in worship,

> > 4. the music to be sung,

> > 5. the use of drama, dance, and other art forms.[5]

Pastors do not control the worship of the congregation by themselves! Presbyterian orders of worship are to be approved by session with the few stated responsibilities limited to the pastor alone. Such a limitation is good for the congregation, for it prevents pastors from imposing their will upon the people and encourages dialogue about changes in the ordering of worship.

Nothing can be more disruptive to most congregations today than changes in our worship. We come with rather clear expectations and we tend to dislike anything that challenges us to do what we do not expect, no matter how ancient the practice or how much Calvin or other people in the past have commended it. Perhaps because many orders of service today are simply the products of long use without any particular theological or biblical rationale, changes to these orders are often seen as a threat by many people who have falsely associated the way we have always done it with the way God intends it to be done!

The basic structure for Presbyterian worship since the Westminster Assembly has been a time of gathering, the hearing of the Word, responding to that Word, and being sent forth into the world. These four actions gather together all we do. Gathering includes a call to worship, a hymn of praise, perhaps a choral introit, a prayer of confession and assurance of pardon, perhaps a time of greeting one another before moving to hearing the Word. During this central part of the worship, the Scripture is read, sung, and proclaimed in the sermon. The response to the Word is in the sacraments, which seal the Word, and in actions such as our prayers of dedication of ourselves, prayers of thanksgiving, a confession of faith, and a hymn of dedication. Sending out may include the offering, announcement, prayers of intercession for the world, and a charge and benediction. Any disruption of this order should be thought out carefully, discussed thoroughly by session, and done only after consultation with the Directory for Worship.

Notes

1. *Book of Order,* W-3.3202.
2. *Book of Order,* G-10.0102, d.
3. *Book of Order,* G-10.0302, c.
4. *Book of Order,* W-1.4004.
5. *Book of Order,* W-1.4005.

Questions for Discussion and Reflection

1. What most annoys you when you see a change in the worship design?
2. How familiar are you with the *Book of Common Worship?* Would you like to know it better?
3. How do you see the balance between freedom and order in the worship of your congregation?
4. How many different hymnals are used in your congregation? Do they lead to greater variety in worship?
5. Do you think that the session of your congregation abides by the rules in the Directory for Worship?
6. What is your favorite hymn or hymns? What makes them special to you?
7. Do you think that your pastor uses the new *Book of Common Worship?* What makes you think that?

7

The Worship Wars:
Traditional or Contemporary

As we begin the twenty-first century, one of the most striking features of church life, which seems to be in every denominational tradition and ethnic group, is the conflict over style of worship. In congregation after congregation, large and small, there are groups that often seem to be at war with each other over these differences, and the pastor and other church leaders find themselves in the middle trying to mediate the disputes and arrange for compromises. Usually there is one group that resists all change (the traditionalists), insisting that the way it has always been done is the only way in which proper worship should be conducted. They are uncomfortable with the introduction of nearly any musical instrument other than the organ, piano, or flute and offended by applause or movement in the service, no matter how slight. They are frequently bothered by any open display of emotion, whether tears or laughter. They have a clear sense of the meaning of the sacred and are prepared to resist anything that does not meet their standard. Since these people are often long-time members, they exercise considerable control and financial pressure to resist change.

At the other extreme are those who want to get rid of what they see as outmoded procedures and out-of-date language and to move into the new world of the twenty-first century with pride and enthusiasm. They are dissatisfied with the slow pace of change and may demand a separate service in which they can start from scratch without the trappings of the past to hold them back. They are impatient, but because they are younger and more recent members, they are less likely to hold positions of power. However, they do speak loudly with their feet when they leave for more upbeat congregations, which they believe will more adequately meet their needs and express the spirit in ways that they can understand.

There was a time, only a few decades ago, when worship was very much taken for granted, especially by Presbyterians who were rather proud of their elegant and dignified forms of worship and satisfied with the established patterns. They liked classical music, which reflected a long and rich heritage, and they took for granted the fact that the service would follow a familiar pattern without fail. Even efforts to increase the frequency of Communion beyond the usual four times a year were strongly resisted. By and large, the people were content with Sunday morning. They may have disagreed with something the minister said in a sermon but not with the rest of the service. They knew what to expect week after week. Because the liturgy did not vary, they either were satisfied and returned regularly or they were bored and attended only occasionally for special events and on major holidays such as Christmas and Easter. Until the mid 1960s their absence was not really noticed because church attendance among Presbyterians was still growing.

The only exception to this general agreement about the proper way to worship may have been the choice of hymns, most often from *The Presbyterian Hymnal* (1933), when congregations demanded what were deemed "the good old songs." The old songs that some wanted to sing were not medieval or Reformation period chants and so were really not very old. Rather, they were hymns or songs from the late 1800s and early 1900s that came out of the revival movement and included "When the Roll Is Called Up Yonder," "Blessed Assurance," "Bringing in the Sheaves," and "In the Garden." However, others saw these gospel songs as undignified and overly sentimental. Many Presbyterians resisted the reintroduction of these hymns because they felt that they not only reflected poor taste but because many of these folks also associated them with revivals and hence were suspicious of their evangelizing quality, which they felt outmoded. In the interest of propriety, many Presbyterians believed that such revivals were best left to the Baptists or Pentecostals. The conflicts between these groups was sometimes enough to fracture the peace of a congregation.

Then came the 1960s, and things began to change. Church attendance and membership began to decline among Presbyterians and other mainstream Protestants. Some people were angry over efforts to address the pressing social issues of the day, such as civil rights, urban decay, and the war in Vietnam. Others felt the church was far too timid and left out of impatience. Churches began to notice that youth were becoming scarce and that congregations were beginning to show signs of aging.

Many congregations tried to appeal to the dissatisfied young with services called "contemporary." These services were often conducted by a pastor who did not wear a robe. They often were held in a fellowship hall rather than the sanctuary, and the pastor was assisted by musicians who played guitars, flutes, or drums. The music was not from the hymnal but from an alternative songbook, sometimes one that people of the congregation had put together (many times photocopied without proper copyright permissions). The hymns were very much like the popular folk songs of the period, often with a strong message of protest about the Vietnam War or a civil rights theme, such as "We Shall Overcome." Sometimes clapping accompanied the rhythm of the guitars and the service had a sense of excitement. Because it was new, this service took most of the creative energy of the pastor, and the "traditional" service was drained of its energy and often of its youth. Visitors usually would attend the traditional service, and they were quite likely to go away thinking that this congregation was not a very warm or exciting place!

Often, two quite different congregations developed with different styles and sometimes with different understandings of the meaning of the faith. The pastor was often trapped in the gap between these two and had to become a human bridge to prevent open warfare. The traditional congregation felt threatened by the changes made by the contemporary folks, who were disdainful of the traditional service. Sometimes a coffee hour between the two services provided an attempt to build civil relationships between the groups. Once I was a guest preacher in such a congregation. I preached at the contemporary service first, and I was warned to expect to be bored by the traditional service. When I preached at the second service, others apologized for what I must have had to endure in the contemporary service. Here was a congregation ready to be split apart. Only a shared loyalty to a beloved pastor temporarily kept that from happening.

After some years, many of these divided congregations dropped the contemporary service altogether. No matter how many changes were made, the young did not respond very enthusiastically, and the time demand on the pastor (and probably also the musicians) was just too great. Sometimes, the traditional service took on certain features of the newer practices, such as passing the peace, more informal dress, and even a mixing of musical styles. In time, the titles "traditional" and "contemporary" were dropped altogether. The remaining difficulty was that people who wanted no change were still upset by the innovations, and people who looked for more drastic changes were disappointed;

in short, no one was satisfied. Church attendance among Presbyterians and other mainstream Protestants continued to decline across America starting in 1965 and has not let up appreciably since then.

After three decades of decline and the example of rapidly growing mega-churches, most of which were nondenominational, many congregations began to move in earnest to make more drastic changes. Some abandoned the traditional service altogether, inviting those who sought such worship to move on to another congregation. A burst of enthusiasm quite often filled the air as the organ was forsaken or even removed completely. Traditional orders were abandoned, the music took on an up-beat note, and the whole service became very informal. Those who were made to feel unwelcome in their own church often reluctantly fled to safer places where change would not be so drastic, but wounds from the experience of rejection by one's own church are difficult to heal.

The kind of worship service that has emerged in many congregations is quite casual in every way. This is true particularly in the West, where tradition has never played an important role and where membership decline has seemed most obvious. People arrive in shorts, T-shirts, and sandals. Coats and ties, heels and hats are absent except for a few visitors or some traditionalists. The pastor wears an open-necked sport shirt if male, or a skirt or slacks and a blouse if female, to conduct the service, which is rarely done from the pulpit. The pulpit itself is located in the middle of the congregation rather than being set apart in a position of authority. The sermon is often more conversational in tone, as the pastor usually does not use a script and has regular eye contact with the people. When one is looking into people's eyes and seeing their responses, it is impossible for the experience not to become more dialogical.

The order of worship that has tended to emerge in these congregations is composed of a time for gathering and involves the singing of several praise songs. Then there are announcements, often made by many different people from within the congregation. A time of prayer includes passing a microphone so that people are able to express their petitions and intercessions aloud and be heard by everyone. Following this time of prayer, the pastor reads Scripture and preaches. An offering is received and more praise songs conclude the service. The atmosphere for such worship is high with energy, full of enthusiasm and warmth. Often the words to the hymns are projected on screens around the walls. Sometimes even major themes of the sermon are projected, and when this is done in careful consultation with the preacher, the pictures can reinforce the spoken word. Among people who have been raised with television, this extensive use of the visual material is very important. These services are more child-friendly because of the informality. Quite often church school classes are held after the children have been in worship for the first part of the service. The sounds of children and their movements add life to the worship experience, providing a sense of the whole church as family.

What is lacking in such services is a clear sense of continuity with any long-standing tradition. The services have little or no connection with any denominational heritage; a visitor would be hard put to recognize to which denomination this congregation was connected. The music is all newly written, and the great treasury of hymnody within the Protestant tradition is lost almost entirely. The great prayers of the ages are also gone, and prayer time lacks the elegance of classic English inasmuch as it is replaced by a kind of chatty, almost casual, attitude toward God. Except for the reading of Scripture, the whole service seems to exist in a historical vacuum as if no one from the past had ever had anything wise to say. Young people who are being raised in these services will never become acquainted with the Protestant tradition of worship.

The issue of musical taste is paramount in the division between those who seem to prefer the contemporary service and those who stick to a traditional one where Bach and Brahms are still played and sung and the thunderous notes of a grand organ lead the singing. The newer songs are easily sung while the traditional hymns may require some musical ability to sing. Just as far more recordings of popular music, rock, rhythm and blues, and other contemporary forms are sold than of classical music, so the taste of North Americans has been captured by television. In my own experience, I remember very well how disdainfully "In the Garden" was used as a parody by seminary professors who caricatured its bad poetry and overly sweet sentimentality of musical style. I accepted this critique until I realized that the song was one that my mother and father used to sing together at the piano. That song had great emotive quality for me, and no appeal to good taste could change my attachment to it. The same can probably be said about some of the praise songs being used today if they reflect what is happening in the lives of people outside the church. The traditional hymn style of music is simply not heard much in any place but the church. To people who were not raised in the church, such hymns may seem quaint at best and irrelevant at worst.

Taste is nearly impossible to judge, but nearly everyone knows how they feel about particular music. The story is told in many forms about the disruption of business establishments, including shopping malls and restaurants, which were being overwhelmed by young people whose presence and high noise level were driving away other customers. The management decided to play only "oldies" mixed with classic music and the teenagers quickly left.

Many adults find praise songs musically tiring and believe that most of them have little to say, making their appeal as they do on the basis of endless repetition of words and musical phrases. Of course, one could level the same criticism of Taizé music! More important, however, because they reflect a single mood, that of praise, they may also miss the variety of needs present on a given Sunday: grief, weariness, discouragement, disappointment, or dissatisfaction with life.

The other element missing in this kind of service is intellectual content. A sermon preached off the cuff without notes, even if carefully prepared, may move the people but is likely to be more shallow than one that has been carefully crafted by using a printed manuscript. For Presbyterians especially, the lack of content is particularly inappropriate. Our denomination requires our ministers to be familiar with both Hebrew and Greek so that they can exegete the Scriptures properly and present a sermon that treats Scripture with care and accuracy. Every major denomination shares a respect for intellectual preparation of its pastors. It is doubtful that the pastor who takes no notes into the service as a mark of pride can be a scholar of Scripture in preaching.

More than anything else, the sheer repetition of the contemporary service is a factor that makes it necessary for those who plan the services to try harder and harder to prevent boredom in worship. Because these services rarely follow the church year except for the major festivals like Christmas and Easter, change of pace is harder to introduce. More variety of music might be called for, yet most of these services seem stuck with praise songs that seem to ignore most of the gospel in favor of endless repetition of phrases such as "we praise you," "we glorify your holy name," "you are mighty, Lord." The theme of praise is natural, but it tends to crowd out other themes, including repentance, thanksgiving, confession, and petition. Frequently, even the name of Jesus is omitted.

In spite of the weaknesses of what we call contemporary worship, it does appeal to people who were raised with the stimulation of television. The noise level, which may be uncomfortable for older persons, is exactly what people under fifty tend to like. Thus, the chief value of these services is that they appeal to the very people who are otherwise obviously missing from many of our churches. Such services are attractive, and people seem to respond with enthusiasm.

The dilemma faced by every congregation is how much to cling to from the past and how far to go in embracing the new. In her important book *Reaching Out without Dumbing Down,* Marva Dawn states the case boldly. She holds out the twin goals of maintaining faithfulness to the gospel and appeal to the mind as well as attracting people who are bored and seeking more stimulation in worship.

Even the names we give to these two kinds of worship are misleading. How traditional in fact are our services? They have changed in many ways over the last thirty years. They no longer use King James English, and many people who attend are quite likely to be dressed far more informally than their predecessors of the 1950s. In the same way, the word "contemporary" is only partially correct. These services retain elements structured quite like the traditional ones, and the faith of the ages is being presented and traditions such as baptism and Holy Communion are being carried on.

If our goal is to increase attendance and membership, there are other forms of worship to consider which could also be called contemporary. Some of these are old forms that have become popular in recent years, but because they are not part of our Presbyterian tradition, at least as that tradition has taken shape in the United States, they may seem foreign or novel. The use of silence and quiet chanting such as that practiced by the Taizé community in France has become quite common. These Taizé services also appeal to younger people who flock to the monastic community in France by the thousands. Taizé services may be held at times other than Sunday morning or they may be incorporated into the regular Sunday service. Some Taizé chants are, in fact, included in *The Presbyterian Hymnal.* These easily singable chants are a form of sung prayer, for nearly all are in the form of prayer. They are also repetitious and therefore easily followed without a songbook in hand. They tend to vary in theme more than praise songs and have a more well-rounded and scripturally centered theology.

The periods of quiet characteristic of Taizé worship enable worshipers to experience a sense of the awesome presence of God. Often the accompaniment that is provided is also varied so that different instruments may be used, from flute to keyboard, to violin or horn. This variety keeps the music interesting. Because ecumenical groups are often sponsors of Taizé services, Roman Catholic and Protestant worshipers are brought together. Attendance is testimony to the fact that people under the age of fifty are touched by these services. Silence is another source of appeal to those whose lives are over-stimulated and who seek relief from the constant bombardment of words.

Another form of worship that is somewhat unfamiliar to Presbyterians is the weekly celebration of Holy Communion. Because the sacrament is tactile, involving the various senses of touch, taste, smell, sight, and movement, it also appeals to younger people. Those congregations with weekly celebrations of the Lord's Supper often discover that objections by seniors are matched by enthusiasm from the young. It is no accident that many young people, attracted by the chanting, the incense, the candles, processions, and the ancient character of the liturgy, have deserted Protestant worship to become Eastern Orthodox. As people without much tradition in their lives and with very few symbols or rituals left to them, the young are hungry for what the Eastern Orthodox liturgy provides. The nonverbal elements in this worship appeal to the various senses and move the worshiper from head to heart. Yet, one would not call such worship contemporary!

Perhaps the whole notion of dividing worship into contemporary and traditional is beside the point. All worship partakes in qualities of both, and both are necessary. In order for worship to be genuinely Christian, it must bear the ancient story, which is a long and essential tradition. All worship must be relevant to the setting in which it takes place and relevant to the lives of the people who attend. It must use the idioms of the time. Sanctified, "holy" language and symbols that no one recognizes, music no one can sing, and rituals that are difficult to interpret do not bring glory to God.

Certain requirements are necessary for all good worship, without which worship will be lacking. There must, for example, be a balance between the use of the mind and the need for a sense of mystery. Those who worship need to learn something about the faith and its application to their lives, but they also need to be lifted above the ordinary to experience a sense of the holy and its mystery. These two are very different attitudes, but both belong in worship whether or not the service is traditional or contemporary. All worship should likewise be composed both of a sense of festival and celebration and opportunities to examine the conscience, so that people grasp the joy of God's love and are caught up with each other in a community of love, but at the same time are aware of their failings, their need for grace, and their call to be more than they have yet been.

To meet these four needs—relevance, mystery, celebration, and contemplation—all worship should meet the following tests:

First: All worship must be, in some sense, contemporary: it must be made up of the elements of the lives of the people and relate to their tastes in a way that they can accept and appreciate. The musical heritage of Protestant worship has changed considerably throughout the ages, from the Genevan Psalter and the Lutheran Chorale, to more recent hymns, and now to the musical genres of this century. Whether it is the music of Taizé, the Iona community, or the music that is called praise songs, this music sounds contemporary. Modern symphonic music does not sound like Bach any longer but more like Bernstein or Howard Hanson. It uses the saxophone and newer, electronic instruments to produce a new sound. We must not expect eighteenth- or nineteenth-century hymns to be instantly beloved by people for whom they are an alien form. Truly contemporary music will use variety, including so called "traditional" hymnody but perhaps sung to a drumbeat. After all, Queen Elizabeth was reported to have said of Genevan Psaltry, "I hate these Genevan jigs." Obviously the syncopation was already present. We are not forsaking our own tradition when we use guitars or drums in worship.

Second: The language of worship must make sense to those who attend worship. Whether it is the prayer language or even the selection of Scripture, the language used in worship must have direct meaning for twenty-first-century people. Lovely prayers with great poetry may have to give way to prayers of intimacy and immediacy in order for them to become truly the prayers of the people. When the people begin to pray in their own language, any sacrifice of elegance is offset by the benefit of allowing those who have gathered to express their true feelings. A sermon preached in the midst of the people can be a direct way of addressing them and responding to their needs. It may not be as biblically sound in its interpretation, but it may cause people to be touched by the Holy Spirit, and that is well worth the price of some lack of intellectual sophistication.

Third: All worship must meet the need of people today for intimate connections with one another. Loneliness and isolation are two of the most destructive plagues of our time in history. People have very few occasions when they can be fully present with others. Our infatuation with technology may have robbed us of human connection. The cell phone, the Internet, and e-mail are three good examples that connect us without really helping us to meet one another. Whether in small groups that gather for prayer and study and sharing of life, or in the larger gathering of the whole community for public worship on Sundays, worship takes place wherever two or three are gathered together in Christ's name. The spiritual nourishment that comes from such gatherings may be in direct relationship to the degree to which people are respected for who they are, welcomed as they are, and taken seriously as individuals. Sitting passively staring at the back of the neck of the person in the pew ahead has very little to do with the longing for community.

Fourth: All worship must use symbols of various sorts, both verbal and nonverbal, to communicate the gospel. Whether it is the outstretched hand offering the peace of Christ, or the passing of the friendship pad recording attendance, or even sharing in the collection of the morning offering, we are connected to each other through the use of symbols. Protestants have surrendered our symbols too easily, trusting too much in our intellectual aptitude and reducing worship to words. We are also connected to a long and ancient past whenever we witness a baptism or share in the breaking of bread and drinking of the cup. Such symbolic actions are rooted in our past, but they speak to people today who feel stained by their own actions and need a sense of cleansing and to people who are starving for God's presence in the midst of the glut of material goods. Baptism and the Lord's Supper are powerful symbolic actions and need to be made the most of in order for our worship to be complete.

Fifth: All worship needs to involve the senses, but especially the sense of sight. Pastors and other worship leaders need to work at providing variety in the worship space so that people can use their eyes as vehicles for seeing as well as hearing the Word. They can do this by using banners and paraments, which are ancient visual tools, but also by using contemporary visual aids such as slides, film, or PowerPoint. The words to hymns and prayers can be projected on the walls or on screens, and since most people today do not read music, the words will be sufficient for most worshipers. A PowerPoint presentation can accompany the sermon, at least once in a while. People are much more likely to remember what they see than what they only hear.

Sixth: All worship today must be "seeker" friendly. Many people who come as visitors do not understand the instructions printed in the bulletin, nor do they understand how to use a hymnal. Some bring with them a particular musical tradition. Worship leaders need to make worship as comfortable as possible for them, providing them with as many aids as possible so that they can follow along with minimal anxiety. For many of them, the act of entering a church is frightening. They worry that they will make a mistake, that they will not be dressed correctly or know the proper language. Pastors must do a far better job than usual to put them at ease.

Seventh: All worship must make the connection with daily life and send the people forth to live as Christians more effectively. If worship stops with the benediction, it has failed the test of relevance, and it doesn't matter how lovely or classic or even how lively it has been. In other words, some elements in the service should lead the congregation to be more dissatisfied with evil, more determined to make a difference in their lives, more empowered to do something noble, more at peace with God. These are the real tests of all good worship.

Questions for Discussion and Reflection

1. Do you normally attend a service of worship that is called contemporary? If so, why do you choose that style?
2. What elements of the modern world speak loudest to you of God?
3. Consider your response to music of the following different styles:
   a. classic: "The Church's One Foundation"
   b. medieval: "Of the Father's Love Begotten"
   c. Reformation: "I Greet Thee Who My Sure Redeemer Art"
   d. modern—praise songs: "Open My Eyes, Lord"
   e. nineteenth century: "Just as I Am"
   f. modern—Taizé: "Hear Our Prayer, O Lord"
   g. modern—Iona: "The Summons"
   h. African American spirituals: "Wade in the Water"
   i. modern—new hymns: "God of the Sparrow"
   j. modern—new hymns from the third world: "We are Singing" (Siyahamba)

   Which of these styles speaks most clearly to you?

4. How do you respond, deep in your heart of hearts, to the use of nonverbal symbols in worship (sharing the peace, bulletin art, liturgical dance, banners, and the like)?
5. Is there a part of worship to which you feel alien? What is it?
6. How do you respond to times of silence in worship?
7. What difference does it make to you whether the pastor preaches from the pulpit or from a place in the midst of the people?
8. Does applause in worship seem appropriate to you? Why or why not?

Resources for Presbyterian Worship

Denominational Resources

Presbyterians have produced great resources for worship. Pastors and sessions need to be familiar with these and use them to see how helpful they are before turning to resources from other sources. Our denominational worship materials are diverse and can be adapted in most congregations with a little imagination. The following are some of the best tools available:

Book of Common Worship. Office of Theology and Worship, Presbyterian Church (U.S.A.). Louisville: Westminster John Knox Press, 1993. (The source book for our liturgies with the wonderful addition of a great translation of the Psalter for singing or speaking responsively.)

Book of Occasional Services: A Liturgical Resource: Supplementing the Book of Common Worship. Office of Theology and Worship, Presbyterian Church (U.S.A.). Louisville: Geneva Press, 1999.

Book of Order (especially the Directory for Worship). Louisville: Office of the General Assembly, Presbyterian Church (U.S.A.), 2000. (Our constitutional guide for how we conduct worship with mandatory regulations and recommendations.)

The Hymnbook. Louisville: Presbyterian Church (U.S.A.), Reformed Church in America, Cumberland Presbyterian Church, 1955.

The Mission Yearbook for Prayer & Study. Mission Education and Promotion Team, Congregational Ministries Publishing, Presbyterian Church (U.S.A.). Louisville: Witherspoon Press, 2005. (Lectionary readings, hymn suggestions, and other worship materials in addition to a guide for intercession.)

The Presbyterian Hymnal: Hymns, Psalms, and Spiritual Songs. Office of Theology and Worship, Presbyterian Church (U.S.A.). Louisville: Westminster/John Knox Press, 1990. (The most recent official hymnal with a great collection of the hymns of our tradition and the addition of new hymns and spirituals and service music.)

The Presbyterian Hymnal Companion. McKim, LindaJo H. Louisville: Westminster John Knox, 1993. (The story of every hymn in the hymnal, how it came to be written, something about the author, and notes about the hymn tune.)

Sing the Faith: New Hymns for Presbyterians. Louisville: Geneva Press, 2003.

Resources from Other Denominations Related to PC(USA)

Berthier, Jacques. *Music from Taizé.* Chicago: G.I.A. Publications, 1978.

Book of Common Order of the Church of Scotland. Edinburgh, Scotland: St. Andrews Press, 1994. (The Scottish equivalent of our *Book of Common Worship* with very contemporary prayers.)

The Book of Worship of the United Church of Christ. New York: United Church Office of Life and Leadership, 1986. (Excellent resource to enhance our own BCW. It contains orders for the blessing of a new home and for other special occasions: thanksgiving for the adoption of a child and recognition of a divorce.)

Duck, Ruth and Michael G. Bausch. *Everflowing Streams: Songs for Worship.* Cleveland: Pilgrim Press, 1989.

The Iona Community. *Iona Abbey Worship Book.* Glasgow, Scotland: Wild Goose Publications, 2001. (Worship for the Iona Community in Scotland.)

The New Century Hymnal. United Church of Christ. Cleveland, Ohio: Pilgrim Press, 1996. (The most rigorous of all hymnals in its use of inclusive language; contains several fine examples of new words to old hymns.)

Psalter Hymnal. Christian Reformed Church. Grand Rapids, MI: Baker Book House, 1954.

Rejoice in the Lord. Reformed Church in America. Grand Rapids, MI: William B. Eerdmans Publishing Co., 1998.

Shawchuck, Norman and Rueben P. Job. *A Guide to Prayer for All Who Seek God.* Nashville, TN: Upper Room Books, 2003. (An excellent devotional guide.)

Communauté de Taizé. *Praise God: Common Prayer at Taizé.* Translated by Emily Chisolm. New York: Oxford University Press, 1977. (The creative worship resource for this ecumenical community.)

The United Methodist Hymnal. Nashville, TN: United Methodist Publishing House, 1989. (A large collection of hymns and worship materials.)

A Wee Worship Book. John Bell ed. Glasgow, Scotland: Wild Goose Publications, 1999. (A collection of liturgical resources from the Iona Community.)

Books about Presbyterian Worship

Baird, Charles. *The Presbyterian Liturgies: Historical Sketches.* Grand Rapids, MI: Baker Book House,1993.

Byars, Ronald. *The Future of Protestant Worship: Beyond the Worship Wars.* Louisville: Westminster John Knox Press, 2002.

Daniels, Harold, Daniel Westler, Cynthia Jarvis, et. al., eds. *Worship in the Community of Faith.* Richmond, VA: The Joint Office of Worship, 1982.

Hageman, Howard. *Pulpit and Table.* Richmond, VA: John Knox Press, 1962.

Noren, Carol M. *What Happens Sunday Morning.* Louisville: Westminster/John Knox Press, 1992.

Rice, Howard and James C. Huffstutler. *Reformed Worship.* Louisville: Geneva Press, 2001.

Schwanda, Tom. *Celebrating God's Presence: The Transforming Power of Public Worship.* Grand Rapids, MI: CRC Publications, 1995.

Wolfe, Janet. *Reformed and Ecumenical: A Comparative History of the Changes in the Texts of Worship Resources Developed Since 1961, in the Presbyterian Church (U.S.A.) in the Light of Ecumenical Models of Worship.* Ann Arbor, MI: UMI Dissertation Service, 1998.

Other Important Books about Worship

The Book of Common Worship. The Church of South India. New York and Madras: Oxford University Press, 1963.

Duck, Ruth. *Bread for the Journey, Resources for Worship.* New York: Pilgrim Press, 1982. (Prayers and liturgies for many different occasions.)

Job, Reuben and Norman Shawchuck. *A Guide to Prayer for All God's People.* Nashville, TN: Upper Room Books, 1998.

Uniting in Worship. Melbourn, Australia: Uniting Church Press, 1988.

White, James. *Introduction to Christian Worship.* Nashville, TN: Abingdon Press, 1980.

Resources on Church Architecture

AIA Journal, American Institute of Architects
1735 New York Avenue, NE, Washington, DC 20006

Faith and Form, Guild for Religious Architecture
1777 Church Street, NW, Washington, DC 20036

Stained Glass Association of America
10009 East 62nd Street, Raytown, MO 64133

Books on Church Architecture

Bieler, Andre. *Architecture in Worship.* Philadelphia: Westminster Press, 1964.

Debuyst, Frédéric. *Modern Architecture and Christian Celebration.* Richmond, VA: John Knox Press, 1967.

Sovik, Edward A. *Architecture for Worship.* Minneapolis, MN: Augsburg Publishing House, 1973.

White, James F. *Protestant Worship and Church Architecture.* New York: Oxford University Press, 1964.

Art and Worship

Bevan, Edwyn. *Symbolism and Belief.* Boston: Beacon Press, 1939.

Chinn, Nancy. *Spaces for Spirit: Adorning the Church.* Chicago: Liturgy Training Publications, 1998.

Davies, Horton and Hugh Davies. *Sacred Art in a Secular Century.* Collegeville, MN: Liturgical Press, 1978.

Richardson, Cyril. "Some Reflections on Liturgical Art," *Union Seminary Quarterly Review,* VIII, Spring, 1953.

Troeger, Thomas H. "Art in Worship: The Integrity of Form and Faith," *Reformed Liturgy and Music,* Vol. XVII, Number 3 (Summer, 1983).

Van der Leeuw, Gerardus. *Sacred and Profane Beauty: The Holy in Art.* Nashville, TN: Abingdon Press, 1963.

Dance and Worship

Adams, Doug. *Congregational Dancing in Christian Worship*. Austin, TX: The Sharing Company, 1976.

Davies, J. G. *Liturgical Dance: An Historical, Theological and Practical Handbook*. Philadelphia: Fortress Press, 1985.

Deitering, Carolyn. *The Liturgy as Dance and the Liturgical Dancer*. New York: Crossroad, 1984.

Rock, Judith and Norman Mealy. *Performer as Priest and Prophet: Restoring the Intuitive in Worship Through Music and Dance*. San Francisco: Harper & Row, 1988.

Banners and Vestments

Anderson, Vienna. *Banners, Mobiles, Odds and Ends*. New York: Morehouse-Barlow Co., 1973.

DeBord, Jane. *Banner Designs for Celebrating Christians*. St Louis, MO: Concordia Publishing House, 1984.

Ireland, Marion. *Textile Art in Church*. Nashville, TN: Abingdon Press, 1971.

Nicholls, Thomas. "Improving Liturgical Banners, *Reformed Liturgy and Music* 17:3 (Summer, 1984).

The Worship Wars

Barna, George. *User Friendly Churches: What Christians Need to Know About the Churches People Love to Go to*. Ventura, CA: Regal Books, 1991.

Dawn, Marva. *Reaching Out without Dumbing Down*. Grand Rapids, MI: Wm. B. Eerdmans Publishing Co., 1995.

Long, Thomas G. *Beyond the Worship Wars: Building Vital and Faithful Worship*. Washington, DC: Alban Institute, 2001.

Makeever, Ray. *Dancing at the Harvest*. Minneapolis, MN: Augsburg Press, 1997.

Miller, Donald. *Reinventing American Protestantism: Christianity in the New Millennium*. Berkeley: University of California Press, 1999.

Parker, Alice. *Melodious Accord: Good Singing in Church*. Chicago: Liturgy Training Publications, 1991.

Senn, Frank. *New Creation: A Liturgical Worldview*. Minneapolis: Augsburg Fortress Publishing, 2000.

Webber, Robert. *Blended Worship: Achieving Substance and Relevance in Worship*. Peabody, MA: Hendrickson, 1996.

Wren, Brian. *Praying Twice: The Music and Words of Congregational Song*. Louisville: Westminster John Knox Press, 2000.